Global Forum on Transparency and Exchange of Information for Tax Purposes Peer Reviews: Lesotho 2016

PHASE 2:
IMPLEMENTATION OF THE STANDARD IN PRACTICE

November 2016
(reflecting the legal and regulatory framework as at August 2016)

OECD
BETTER POLICIES FOR BETTER LIVES

This work is published on the responsibility of the Secretary-General of the OECD. The opinions expressed and arguments employed herein do not necessarily reflect the official views of the OECD or of the governments of its member countries or those of the Global Forum on Transparency and Exchange of Information for Tax Purposes.

This document and any map included herein are without prejudice to the status of or sovereignty over any territory, to the delimitation of international frontiers and boundaries and to the name of any territory, city or area.

Please cite this publication as:
OECD (2016), *Global Forum on Transparency and Exchange of Information for Tax Purposes Peer Reviews: Lesotho 2016: Phase 2: Implementation of the Standard in Practice*, OECD Publishing.
http://dx.doi.org/10.1787/9789264266148-en

ISBN 978-92-64-26613-1 (print)
ISBN 978-92-64-26614-8 (PDF)

Series: Global Forum on Transparency and Exchange of Information for Tax Purposes Peer Reviews
ISSN 2219-4681 (print)
ISSN 2219-469X (online)

Corrigenda to OECD publications may be found on line at: *www.oecd.org/publishing/corrigenda*.

Table of Contents

About the Global Forum

The Global Forum on Transparency and Exchange of Information for Tax Purposes is the multilateral framework within which work in the area of tax transparency and exchange of information is carried out by over 130 jurisdictions, which participate in the Global Forum on an equal footing.

The Global Forum is charged with in-depth monitoring and peer review of the implementation of the international standards of transparency and exchange of information for tax purposes. These standards are primarily reflected in the 2002 OECD Model Agreement on Exchange of Information on Tax Matters and its commentary, and in Article 26 of the OECD Model Tax Convention on Income and on Capital and its commentary as updated in 2004. The standards have also been incorporated into the UN Model Tax Convention.

The standards provide for international exchange on request of foreseeably relevant information for the administration or enforcement of the domestic tax laws of a requesting party. Fishing expeditions are not authorised but all foreseeably relevant information must be provided, including bank information and information held by fiduciaries, regardless of the existence of a domestic tax interest or the application of a dual criminality standard.

All members of the Global Forum, as well as jurisdictions identified by the Global Forum as relevant to its work, are being reviewed. This process is undertaken in two phases. Phase 1 reviews assess the quality of a jurisdiction's legal and regulatory framework for the exchange of information, while Phase 2 reviews look at the practical implementation of that framework. Some Global Forum members are undergoing combined – Phase 1 and Phase 2 – reviews. The Global Forum has also put in place a process for supplementary reports to follow-up on recommendations, as well as for the ongoing monitoring of jurisdictions following the conclusion of a review. The ultimate goal is to help jurisdictions to effectively implement the international standards of transparency and exchange of information for tax purposes.

All review reports are published once approved by the Global Forum and they thus represent agreed Global Forum reports.

For more information on the work of the Global Forum on Transparency and Exchange of Information for Tax Purposes, and for copies of the published review reports, please refer to www.oecd.org/tax/transparency and www.eoi-tax.org.

Abbreviations

AMATM	African Tax Administration Forum Agreement on Mutual Assistance in Tax Matters
AML	Anti-money laundering
CBL	Central Bank of Lesotho
CDD	Customer due-diligence
CFT	Combating the financing of terrorism
DTA	Double taxation agreements
ESAAMLG	Eastern and Southern Africa Anti-Money Laundering Group
EOI	Exchange of information
EOI Manual	Exchange of Information Standard Operating Procedure
EUR	Euro
FI Act	Financial Institutions Act of 2012
FIU	Financial Intelligence Unit
IAU	Internal Affairs Unit
ITD	International Treaty Development
KYC	know-your-customer
LRA	Lesotho Revenue Authority
LSL	Basotho Loti (official currency in Lesotho)
MLPC Act	Money Laundering and Proceeds of Crime Act 2008
MTICM	Ministry of Trade and Industry, Cooperatives and Marketing
OBFC	One-Stop Business Facilitation Centre
SADC Agreement	Southern African Development Community Agreement on Assistance in Tax Matters
TIEA	Tax information exchange agreement

Executive summary

1. This report summarises the legal and regulatory framework for transparency and exchange of information in Lesotho, as well as the practical implementation of that framework. The international standard, which is set out in the Global Forum's Terms of Reference to Monitor and Review Progress Towards Transparency and Exchange of Information, is concerned with the availability of relevant information within a jurisdiction, the competent authority's ability to gain timely access to that information, and in turn, whether that information can be effectively exchanged on a timely basis with its exchange of information partners. The assessment of effectiveness in practice has been performed in relation to a three year period (1 July 2012 through 30 June 2015).

2. Lesotho is a small landlocked country, surrounded by South Africa. It has an area of approximately 30 000 square kilometres and a population of 2 098 000 (latest estimate from 2014). It is a low-income developing economy in which about three-quarters of the people live in rural areas and engage in subsistence agriculture. Lesotho's GDP as at 2015 is about USD 2.6 billion. The economy of Lesotho is closely linked and dependent on the economy of South Africa with 90% of the goods it consumes coming from South Africa. A large economic sector is diamond mining.

3. All relevant entities in Lesotho are subject to comprehensive requirements under commercial, tax, and anti-money laundering laws to maintain and have available relevant ownership, accounting and bank information. Such information is also available for exchange of information ("EOI") purposes. All relevant entities are required to register with and report any changes of its owners to government authorities in Lesotho. There is no legislation in Lesotho regarding bearer shares. The issuance of bearer shares in Lesotho is effectively impeded through the mechanisms under the Companies Act which ensure that ownership information of all shares are available since details of any share transfer must be recorded and reported to government authorities, and that persons can only claim their legal title to the shares if they are listed on the share register. These rules also appear adequate to ensure the availability of identification information of all holders of share warrants which may be issued by public companies if allowed under the

companies' articles of association and approved by the Lesotho authorities. However, as there are also no express provisions in the laws requiring ownership information to be retained specifically in respect of all share warrants to bearer, there remains some uncertainty as to whether the mechanisms are sufficiently robust to ensure the availability of information identifying all holders of share warrants to bearer. It is therefore recommended that Lesotho should take necessary measures to ensure that robust mechanisms are in place to identify the owners of share warrants to bearer or eliminate companies' ability to issue such share warrants.

4. Lesotho did not conduct regular oversight of the availability of ownership and identity on companies during the review period. However, after the review period the Registrar of Companies conducted a re-registration programme, in which all domestic and foreign (external) companies had to update their corporate information, including that of directors and owners. After completion of this programme, there were 17 029 private companies, 504 public companies and 58 foreign (external) companies struck off from the Companies Registry and a new systematic oversight programme was created to be implemented from 2016 on. Lesotho should monitor the implementation of this new oversight programme and exercise its enforcement powers as appropriate to ensure that ownership and identity information for domestic and foreign (external) companies is available in practice.

5. Further, Lesotho did not conduct any regular oversight during the review period to verify compliance with the obligations to keep ownership and identity information for partnerships, all types of trust and societies. Therefore, Lesotho should put in place an oversight programme to ensure compliance with the obligations to maintain ownership and identity information of partnerships, all types of trust and societies, and exercise its enforcement powers as appropriate to ensure that such information is available in practice.

6. Lesotho's tax and commercial laws impose the obligation to keep adequate accounting information including underlying documentation for a minimum of five years in line with the standard in respect of almost all entities. The Lesotho Revenue Authority ("LRA") monitors compliance with the accounting recordkeeping obligations prescribed by the tax laws but this supervision is limited to registered taxpayers, which include domestic and foreign (external) companies, partnerships and trusts deriving income in Lesotho. There is a regular oversight programme in place to ensure that the accounting requirements prescribed by the Income Tax Act are complied with. However, trusts that only receive foreign-source income and where the settlor is a non-resident are not covered by the oversight that the LRA conducts. It is, therefore, recommended that the LRA puts in place a comprehensive oversight programme to ensure compliance with and enforcement of

the obligation to maintain reliable accounting records and underlying documents for all relevant entities and arrangements.

7. In respect of banks, legal requirements to ensure the availability of banking information are based on banking and anti-money laundering ("AML) laws, which are in line with the standard. During the review period the Central Bank of Lesotho ("CBL") conducted yearly audits on all commercial banks in Lesotho. In the course of these audits the CBL did not supervise in detail AML obligations during the review period as the supervision of these obligations is conducted by the Financial Intelligence Unit ("FIU"). The FIU however, did not conduct any oversight of AML obligations during the review period. Consequently, no enforcement measures were applied for non-compliance of AML obligations by banks regarding their customer due diligence requirements.

8. The Lesotho competent authority has broad access powers to obtain and provide requested information held by persons within its territorial jurisdiction. Information gathering powers which can be used for domestic purposes can also be used for EOI purposes regardless of whether there is a domestic tax interest. Lesotho has in place enforcement provisions to compel the production of information, including criminal sanctions and search and seizure power. Neither bank nor professional secrecy provisions in Lesotho's laws interfere with the access powers of the competent authority. Lesotho's law does not require notification of the taxpayer prior to exchange of information. There are also no specific legal provisions allowing the taxpayer to appeal the exchange of information. During the review period, the Lesotho competent authority was able to access information to reply to EOI requests concerning banking and property information.

9. Lesotho has in total 14 EOI relationships with relevant partners through five double taxation agreements ("DTAs"), two tax information exchange agreements (TIEAs), the African Tax Administration Forum Agreement on Mutual Assistance in Tax Matters ("AMATM") and the Southern African Development Community Agreement on Assistance in Tax Matters ("SADC Agreement"), all except one of which are in line with the standard. This exception concerns the earlier signed DTA with the Seychelles which has been re-negotiated to be in line with the standard and which is pending signing. Lesotho should conclude the DTA negotiated with Seychelles to bring all EOI arrangements in line with the standard. Further, there are two DTAs pending approval since 2010 and 2011 and Lesotho should ensure that its EOI agreements brought into force expeditiously.

10. All of Lesotho's EOI agreements have confidentiality provisions to ensure that the information exchanged will be disclosed only to persons authorised by the agreements. Feedback from peers indicates that there have been no issues with confidentiality as it relates to EOI requests. All EOI

agreements also ensure that the contracting parties are not obliged to provide information which is subject to legal professional privilege. The term "professional secret" is not defined in the EOI agreements but as described under B.1.5, professional privilege in Lesotho is covered under common law, which is in line with the standard and has never prevented Lesotho from exchanging information on account of objections founded on professional secrecy.

11. Overall, Lesotho has a legal and regulatory framework in place that ensures the availability, access and exchange of all relevant information for tax purposes in accordance with the international standard. During the period under review (1 July 2012 – 30 June 2015) Lesotho received two requests from one jurisdiction. Although the number is limited, the EOI requests covered a range of ownership, accounting, banking and property information. Lesotho has provided information in one case within 90 days and in the other case within 180 days. Some delays have been identified when EOI requests reach Lesotho's competent authority. Lesotho presently only receives requests in hard copies and EOI partners were contacted by the Lesotho competent authority to inform them on the most appropriate way to send EOI requests. The resources currently allocated to the International Treaty Development (ITD) Section are adequate to deal with the present workload. Feedback from peers indicates that they were generally satisfied with Lesotho's level of co-operation.

12. Lesotho has been assigned a rating for each of the 10 essential elements as well as an overall rating. The ratings for the essential elements are based on the analysis in the text of the report, taking into account the Phase 1 determinations and any recommendations made in respect of Lesotho's legal and regulatory framework and the effectiveness of its exchange of information in practice. On this basis, Lesotho has been assigned the following ratings: Compliant for elements B.1, B.2,C.1, C.2, C.3 and C.4, Largely Compliant for elements A.2, A.3 and C.5 and Partially Compliant for element A.1. In view of the ratings for each of the essential elements taken in their entirety, the overall rating for Lesotho is Largely Compliant.

13. A follow up report on the steps undertaken by the Lesotho to answer the recommendations made in this report should be provided to the PRG by June 2017 and thereafter in accordance with the process set out under the Methodology for the next round of reviews.

Introduction

Information and methodology used for the peer review of Lesotho

14. The assessment of the legal and regulatory framework of Lesotho was based on the international standards for transparency and exchange of information as described in the Global Forum's Terms of Reference to Monitor and Review Progress Towards Transparency and Exchange of Information For Tax Purposes, and was prepared using the Global Forum's Methodology for Peer Reviews and Non-Member Reviews. The assessment was based on the laws, regulations, and exchange of information mechanisms in force or effect as at 22 May 2015, Lesotho's responses to the Phase 1 questionnaire and supplementary questions, other materials supplied by Lesotho, and information supplied by partner jurisdictions.

15. The Phase 2 assessment is based on the laws, regulations and exchange of information mechanisms in force or in effect as at 12 August 2016, Lesotho's responses to the Phase 2 questionnaire, supplementary questions and other materials supplied by Lesotho, information provided by exchange of information partners, and explanations provided by Lesotho during the on-site visit that took place from 22 to 24 February in Maseru, Lesotho. During the on-site visit, the assessment team met with officials and representatives of the Ministry of Finance, LRA, Registrar of Companies, Registrar of Deeds, Central Bank and Financial Intelligence Unit (see Annex 4).

16. The Terms of Reference break down the standards of transparency and exchange of information into 10 essential elements and 31 enumerated aspects under three broad categories: (A) availability of information, (B) access to information, and (C) exchange of information. This review assesses Lesotho's legal and regulatory framework against these elements and each of the enumerated aspects. In respect of each essential element a determination is made that either: *(i)* the element is in place, *(ii)* the element is in place but certain aspects of the legal implementation of the element need improvement, or *(iii)* the element is not in place. These determinations are accompanied by recommendations for improvement where relevant. A summary of findings against those elements is set out at the end of this report. In addition,

to reflect the Phase 2 component, recommendations are made concerning Lesotho's practical application of each of the essential elements and a rating of either: *(i)* compliant, *(ii)* largely compliant, *(iii)* partially compliant, or *(iv)* non-compliant is assigned to each element. An overall rating is also assigned to reflect Lesotho's overall level of compliance with the standards. A summary of findings against those elements is set out at the end of this report.

17. The Phase 1 assessment was conducted by a team which consists of two assessors: Mr. Abdul Gafur, Section Chief of International Tax Cooperation, Directorate General of Taxes, Ministry of Finance of the Republic of Indonesia and Mr. Philip Mensah, Deputy Commissioner, Board and Legal Affairs, Ghana Revenue Authority, Ministries Accra; and Ms. Audrey Chua, a representative of the Global Forum Secretariat.

18. The Phase 2 assessment was conducted by an assessment team who consisted of two expert assessors: Philip Mensah, Deputy Commissioner, Ghana Revenue Authority, Ghana; Abdul Gafur, Section Chief for Exchange of Information, Directorate General of Taxes, Indonesia; and two representatives from the Global Forum Secretariat: Ervice Tchouata and Ana Rodriguez-Calderon. The assessment team assessed the practical implementation and effectiveness of the legal and regulatory framework for transparency and exchange of information and relevant EOI arrangements in Lesotho.

Overview of Lesotho

19. Lesotho is completely surrounded by South Africa and shares its borders with the three of its provinces: Free State, KwaZulu-Natal and Eastern Cape. Lesotho has ten administrative districts,[1] each headed by District Administrators. Maseru is the political and business capital city of Lesotho.

20. It has an area of approximately 30 000 square kilometres and a population of 2 098 000 (latest estimate from 2014). The main ethnic group of its population is Sotho (99.7%) with the remaining population comprising Europeans, Asians and other ethnicities. The official languages are Sesotho and English. Lesotho nationals are referred to as Basotho, and Mosotho in singular. The official currency in Lesotho is the Basotho Loti[2] (LSL) which is fixed on par with the South African Rand.

1. Maseru, Berea, Leribe, ButhaButhe, Mokhotlong, Mafeteng, Mohale'sHoek, Quthing, Qacha's Nek and ThabaTseka.
2. The exchange rate averaged LSL 17.56 to the Euro during the time of the review based on rates listed on www.xe.com. The plural of Loti is Maloti.

21. Lesotho is a low-income developing economy in which about three-quarters of the people live in rural areas and engage in subsistence agriculture. Lesotho's GDP as at 2015 is about USD 2.6 billion. The economy of Lesotho is closely linked and dependent on the economy of South Africa with 90% of the goods it consumes (mostly agricultural) from South Africa, including most agricultural inputs. Government revenue depends heavily on transfers from South Africa. Customs duties from the Southern Africa Customs Union accounted for 29% of government revenue in 2015. The South African Government also pays royalties for water transferred to South Africa from a dam and reservoir system in Lesotho. However, the Lesotho government continues to strengthen its tax system to reduce dependency on customs duties and other transfers. The government plays a large role in the economy as its largest employer and consumption accounting for 39% of GDP in 2013. Lesotho's largest private employer is the textile and garment industry – approximately 36 000 Basotho, mainly women, work in factories producing garments for export to South Africa and the United States. A large economic sector is diamond mining.

General information on the legal system and the taxation system

Governance and the legal system

22. The Lesotho Government is a constitutional monarchy and the sovereign is the Head of State. The Prime Minister is head of government and has executive authority. The sovereign serves a largely ceremonial function and does not possess any executive authority or participate in political initiatives. The Prime Minister heads the Cabinet which is responsible for all government policies and the day-to-day running of the affairs of the state.

23. The hierarchy of laws in Lesotho comprises, from the top, *(i)* the Constitution, *(ii)* international agreements formed with legal effect of statutory law, *(iii)* statutory law, and *(iv)* common law (the Roman-Dutch law and the English Common Law) and customary law, which operates on equal footing.

24. The Constitution is the supreme law in Lesotho and will prevail over any other law that is inconsistent. Statutory law (legislation) is enacted by the Parliament of Lesotho empowered to make laws (s. 70, Constitution of Lesotho). The dual legal system in Lesotho is based on Roman-Dutch law and English Common Law, combined with customary law, all operating together on equal footing. Both the Roman Dutch and English Common law are systems of law which were imported from the then Cape of Good Hope(current Cape Town in South Africa) in the period 1871-84. Customary law consists

of the customs of the Basotho, written and codified in the Laws of Lerotholi. Customary law is applied in the Local Courts.

25. The Constitution provides for an independent judicial system. At the head of the judiciary is the Court of Appeal, followed by the High Court with unlimited jurisdiction in both civil and criminal matters, then the Subordinate Courts (Magistrate Courts) with different categories of limited jurisdiction in civil and criminal matters according to the hierarchy of the magistracy, and then the Judicial Commissioners Courts, the Central Courts and the Local Courts. The latter three courts largely deal with customary law. In addition, there are specialised tribunals that deal with specialised areas of the law in terms of relevant statutes. These include the Revenue Appeals Tribunal which sits as a judicial authority for hearing and deciding appeals against assessments, decisions, rulings, determinations, and directions of the Commissioner General under the Customs and Excise Act 1982, Income Tax Act 1993 and Value Added Tax 2001 (s. 3(1), Revenue Appeals Tribunal Act 2005). It comprises 10 members appointed by the Minister of Finance and Development Planning that must include an experienced judge of the High Court, legal practitioners, chartered accountants and members of the business community with experience in finance, commerce or economic affairs (s. 4). Sittings of the Tribunal may be held at any time necessary (s. 12) and hearings before the Tribunal shall not be open to the public (s. 13(3)). Decisions of the Tribunal are final and conclusive (s. 17(4)), and would be published in a general format without revealing the identity of the appellant (s. 17(3)). Parties dissatisfied with decisions of the Tribunal may also appeal to the High Court and Court of Appeal (s. 19 and 20).

The tax system

26. Lesotho's tax system comprises direct and indirect taxes. Residents are taxed on world-wide income, and non-residents taxed on Lesotho-sourced income. The self-assessment system is used for residents and electing non-residents. Otherwise, withholding taxes are applied on non-residents. Non-residents can elect to file a return. Individual income tax applies to employed and self-employed persons (e.g. sole traders and partners, unincorporated professionals). The applicable rates range between 20% and 30% with a non-refundable tax credit of LSL 6 100 (EUR 349). All companies pay taxes regardless of their legal status (private, public or government-linked). A legal entity, except for partnerships and trusts, is considered a tax resident of Lesotho if it is incorporated or formed under the laws of Lesotho, has its management and control in Lesotho, or undertakes the majority of operations in Lesotho. The Maseru Securities Market was launched in January 2016 but public share ownership and participation remain available through unit trusts.

27. The corporate tax rate is 25% and 10% for manufacturing income. General services income rendered in Lesotho by non-residents is taxed at 10% on the gross amount. Passive income payable to non-residents is taxed at a standard rate of 25% and applies to dividends, interest, royalty, natural resource payment, management and administrative charges. Manufacturing dividends and royalties payable to non-residents are at 15%. Lesotho has a limited capital gains regime which imposes a tax on the gains from disposal of assets by non-residents at 25%. The LRA administers the three laws that govern the tax system – Income Tax Act of 1993, as amended, VAT Act of 2001, and the Customs and Excise Act of 1982. These tax laws are enacted through an Act of Parliament of Lesotho.

Exchange of information for tax purposes

28. Lesotho has been a member of the Global Forum since February 2013. There is no separate law for exchange of information for tax purposes in Lesotho. Domestic law interacts with the international tax agreements according to the Income Tax Act (s. 112), which prescribes that Lesotho may enter into international agreements with other countries on a reciprocal basis for the prevention of fiscal and evasion or avoidance through the Minister of Finance. A double taxation agreement includes an agreement with a foreign government providing for reciprocal administrative assistance in the enforcement of tax liabilities (s. 112(4)). Lesotho has confirmed that this provision is interpreted to cover all international agreements that provides for EOI – DTAs, TIEAs and the AMATM and SADC agreement. The Income Tax Act allows for disclosure of information under such international agreements (s. 202).

29. DTAs and TIEAs have to be signed by the Minister of Finance, ratified by the Minister of Foreign Affairs and then tabled before Parliament in order to enter into force. Lesotho has adopted the procedures followed by the United Kingdom.

Overview of the financial sector and relevant professions

30. Lesotho has a small financial sector that is closely linked to South Africa. It is dominated by subsidiaries of South African financial institutions. There are four commercial banks, three of which are subsidiaries of South African banks and account for over 95% of total loans and deposits. The fourth bank, the Lesotho Post Bank, is government-owned. At the centre of the financial sector in Lesotho is the CBL, which regulates, supervises and administers the Financial Institutions Act of 2012, the Money Lenders Act of 1989, the Insurance Act of 2014, the Payment Systems Act of 2014 and the Credit Reporting Act of 2011. All financial institutions that

want to conduct activities in Lesotho must be licensed or registered with the CBL. The financial institutions in Lesotho are the commercial banks, money-lenders, individual micro-lenders, insurance companies and brokers, foreign exchange bureau, financial leasing companies, credit information bureau, collective investment schemes, and asset management bodies. There are currently 4 banks, 1 foreign exchange agency, 2 collective investment schemes, 27 insurance brokers, 6 insurance companies and 51 money lenders. Lesotho is a member of the Eastern and Southern Africa Anti-Money Laundering Group (ESAAMLG). An evaluation of its AML and combating the financing of terrorism (CFT) regime was conducted by the ESAAMLG and was approved as a first mutual evaluation by its Council of Ministers on 8 September 2011.

Compliance with the Standards

A. Availability of information

Overview

31. Effective exchange of information requires the availability of reliable information. In particular, it requires information on the identity of owners and other stakeholders as well as information on the transactions carried out by entities and other organisational structures. Such information may be kept for tax, regulatory, commercial or other reasons. If such information is not kept or the information is not maintained for a reasonable period of time, a jurisdiction's competent authority[3] may not be able to obtain and provide it when requested. This section of the report describes and assesses Lesotho's legal and regulatory framework for availability of information. It also assesses the effectiveness of this framework in practice.

32. The legal and regulatory framework in Lesotho ensures that ownership information regarding domestic and foreign (external) companies with a nexus to Lesotho is available. The Companies Act requires all companies to provide identity information on all shareholders and directors upon registration with the Registrar of Companies and report any subsequent changes in directors or shareholders. Nominee ownership through voting trusts by trustees are covered by AML obligations and trustees must retain ownership

3. The term "competent authority" means the person or government authority designated by a jurisdiction as being competent to exchange information pursuant to a double tax convention or tax information exchange.

and identity information of the shareholders it represents. The customer due-diligence ("CDD") and know-your-customer ("KYC") obligations under AML laws further ensure the availability of ownership information for companies where company service providers are engaged.

33. The issuance of bearer shares in Lesotho is effectively impeded through the mechanisms under the Companies Act despite there being no explicit prohibition on bearer shares. The existing rules under these laws appear to be sufficient to ensure that ownership information of all shares are available since details of any share transfer must be recorded and reported, and that persons can only claim their legal title to the shares if they are listed on the share register. These rules appear adequate to ensure the availability of identification information of all holders of share warrants which may be issued by public companies if allowed under the companies' articles of incorporation and approved by the Lesotho authorities. Lesotho authorities have also confirmed that no share warrants have been issued by all 628 public companies in Lesotho which represents 2.25% of all companies in Lesotho. However, as there are also no express provisions in the laws requiring ownership information to be retained specifically in respect of all share warrants to bearer, there remains some uncertainty as to whether the mechanisms are sufficiently robust to ensure the availability of information identifying all holders of share warrants to bearer. It is therefore recommended that Lesotho should take necessary measures to ensure that robust mechanisms are in place to identify the owners of share warrants to bearer or eliminate companies' ability to issue such share warrants. No specific investigation was conducted during the review period to find out whether any of the 628 public companies registered in Lesotho issued share warrants to bearer. However, after the review period all companies underwent a re-registration programme with the Commercial Registrar in which all companies had to update ownership information and no bearer shares were encountered.

34. The legal and regulatory framework ensures that ownership information regarding all partnerships is available. All partnerships must be registered in Lesotho to have legal effect, which means registering with the LRA and filing annual income tax return in which ownership information would be available. Partnerships are required to submit information to the Registrar of Deeds on all their partners and report any subsequent changes. The CDD and KYC obligations under AML laws also further ensure the availability of ownership information for partnerships where service providers are engaged. In practice, only the LRA monitors that partnership ownership information is available through the filing of annual tax returns. Tax filing compliance in respect of partnerships was low during the review period and the LRA was unable to produce statistic on penalties imposed to partnerships that failed to file annual tax return. Lesotho is therefore recommended to put in place an oversight programme to ensure compliance with

the obligations to maintain ownership and identity information of partnerships, and exercise its enforcement powers as appropriate to ensure that such information is available in practice.

35. The combination of common law, tax law and AML obligations ensure the availability of identity information on trustees, settlors and beneficiaries in respect of trusts created under Lesotho laws, administered in Lesotho, or in respect of a resident trustee of a foreign trust in Lesotho. In practice, only the LRA monitors that trust ownership and identity information is available through the filing of annual tax returns However, Lesotho was unable to produce statistics on tax filing compliance of trusts during the review period, which in any case, was low for other types of entities, see A.1.3 *Partnerships*. This information could also be available with the service providers but Lesotho authorities did not regularly monitor compliance of AML obligations during the review period and it is therefore unclear the extent to which this information is available with the service providers. Lesotho should monitor the compliance of the legal obligations to maintain ownership and identity information for all types of trusts, and exercise its enforcement powers as appropriate to ensure that such information is available in practice.

36. There is no specific law for the establishment of foundations in Lesotho and based on the features of the entities called "foundations" that exist in Lesotho, it may be concluded that these are not relevant for the work of the Global Forum. In respect of societies registered under the Societies Act, the availability of identity information on the members is ensured through obligations to provide updated information whenever requested by the Register-General. Societies are likely to be of more limited relevance for EOI as they generally don't conduct business. However, the fact that companies and partnerships can register under the Societies Act is enough to require Lesotho to have ownership and identity information of such entities. Lesotho authorities do not have regular oversight to monitor the compliance of obligations under the Societies Act and it is therefore recommended that Lesotho monitors the compliance of the legal obligations to maintain ownership and identity information of entities registered under the Societies Act and exercise its enforcement powers as appropriate to ensure that such information is available in practice.

37. Enforcement provisions to ensure the availability of ownership information appear to be sufficient for domestic companies, foreign (external) companies, partnerships and societies. For trusts, the availability of identity information of trustees, settlors and beneficiaries can be ensured through the combination of common law fiduciary duties and enforcement provisions under tax and AML laws.

38. Lesotho did not regularly monitor the availability of ownership and identity for any relevant entities and arrangements during the review period. In the case of companies however, the Registrar of Companies conducted a re-registration programme, in which all domestic and foreign (external) companies had to update their corporate information, including that of directors and owners. After completion of this programme, there were 17 591 (17 029 private companies, 504 public companies and 58 foreign (external) companies) out of 29 030 companies altogether struck off from the Companies Registry and a new systematic oversight programme was created to be implemented from 2016 on. Lesotho should monitor the implementation of this new oversight programme and exercise its enforcement powers as appropriate to ensure that ownership and identity information for domestic and external companies is available in practice. Moreover, Lesotho did not conduct any oversight to verify compliance with the obligations to keep ownership and identity information for partnerships, all types of trusts and societies. Therefore, Lesotho should put in place an oversight programme to ensure compliance with the obligations to maintain ownership and identity information of partnerships, all types of trusts and societies, and exercise its enforcement powers as appropriate to ensure that such information is available in practice.

39. The accounting record keeping obligations and the enforcement provisions under tax and commercial laws are in line with the standard in respect of all entities except trusts that do not receive taxable income in Lesotho. Lesotho should ensure the availability of accounting records of all trusts in Lesotho even where the trust is not carrying on business or is not subject to tax in Lesotho. The requirements of the legal and regulatory framework to maintain accounting records and underlying documentation are monitored by the LRA in the course of its audit programme. In respect of banks, legal requirements to ensure the availability of banking information are in line with the standard. The availability of identity information on all account-holders and transaction records is ensured through specific provisions in the Financial Institutions Act and accounting and AML rules. Commercial banks are closely monitored by CBL. However, CBL does not supervise in detail AML obligations as supervision of these obligations is conducted by the FIU. The FIU has reported that their compliance division is very new and that no oversight was carried out during the review period. Consequently, no enforcement measures were applied for non-compliance of AML obligations by banks regarding their customer due diligence requirements.

A.1. Ownership and identity information

Jurisdictions should ensure that ownership and identity information for all relevant entities and arrangements is available to their competent authorities.

Companies (ToR[4] A.1.1)

Types of companies

40. Companies are incorporated and registered under the Companies Act 2011 and Companies Regulations 2012. The following types of companies can be established under Lesotho's laws:

- **private companies** – Private companies do not offer its shares to the public and may not have more than 50 members (s. 2, Companies Act). Such companies are identified by having the words "Limited" or "Ltd" and "Proprietary" or "Pty" at the end of the company's name (s. 15(1), Companies Act). As at August 2016, there were 11 228 private companies registered in Lesotho.
- **public companies** – Public companies are defined as any other company that is not a private company (s. 2, Companies Act). This refers to companies that offer its shares to the public and may be quoted on a stock exchange. Such companies are identified by having the word "Limited" or "Ltd" at the end of the company name (s. 15(1), Companies Act). As at August 2016, there were 155 public companies registered in Lesotho.
- **non-profit making companies** – Non-profit making companies are associations that are registered as companies as they operate in the interests of the public or a section of the public and prohibit the payment of dividends to its members. A non-profit company is not obligated to have the word "Limited" at the end of its name (s. 15(2) and (3), Companies Act).As at August 2016, there were 55 non-profit making companies registered in Lesotho.

41. The application process for incorporation takes place at the One-Stop Business Facilitation Centre ("OBFC") of Lesotho, housed within the Registrar of Companies. The Registrar of Companies is the Director of the OBFC. The OBFC comprises ten officials from different agencies that have deployed personnel: Ministry of Trade and Industry, Cooperatives and Marketing, Ministry of Labour and Employment, Ministry of Home Affairs and the LRA. At the OBFC, the incorporation of the company includes the

4. Terms of Reference to Monitor and Review Progress Towards Transparency and Exchange of Information.

registration of the company as a taxpayer. A company is incorporated upon receiving an incorporation certificate and a Tax Identification Number. Upon incorporation, the company can commence general commercial activities in Lesotho subject to specific sector licensing requirements, if any.

Registration in practice

42. In practice, registration can be done in person at the OBFC facilities or through the OBFC's website. Irrespective of which option is chosen, five steps need to be completed for the registration of a company: *(i)* reserve the company name; *(ii)* provide details of registered office and main business office; *(iii)* indicate who the Directors of the company are, and attach consent form for each Director; *(iv)* indicate who the shareholders of the company are; *(v)* payment of fee. Payment of online registrations is done by setting up a pre-paid deposit account with the Ministry of Trade and Industry, Cooperatives and Marketing (MTICM).

43. A copy of the identification documents of the Directors and shareholders needs to be included with the registration application. When the Directors and shareholders are nationals from Lesotho, the OBFC checks that the identification provided (usually a license) is valid and has not expired. Foreigners are required to submit a copy of their passport which has to be certified by a Commissioner of oaths. All documents required upon registration are kept at the OBFC's database, to which the LRA has access.

44. Once all documents are submitted, the OBFC sends them to the LRA for the LRA to assign a taxpayer identification number. Thus, all companies are registered taxpayers. Once the LRA has assigned the taxpayer identification number, the OBFC proceeds to issue a certification of incorporation in which the taxpayer identification number will appear. The entire process takes one business day when done through the OBFC's website and approximately one week when done in person.

Information kept by public authorities

Registrar of companies

45. The Registrar of Companies ("Registrar") is the main public authority that keeps all ownership and identity information of all companies in Lesotho. Such information would include the name and contact details of all current and past directors and shareholders of all companies. This information is collected during companies' incorporation and is regularly updated when there is a change, which is again verified when companies submit its annual report to the Registrar containing this information. In terms of enforcement provisions to ensure companies' compliance with these obligations, the Registrar is

expected to monitor and is authorised to remove any non-compliant company from the Register and/or apply a penalty. The following paragraphs describe the role and responsibilities of the Registrar as well as the incorporation process for companies, which the Registrar administers under the Companies Act and Companies Regulation.

46. The Registrar is an administrative authority under the supervision of the MTICM. The Registrar is responsible to keep in Lesotho a register of companies incorporated or registered in Lesotho (s. 91). In accordance to the Companies Act, information kept on the register was previously available for public access upon payment of the prescribed fee (s. 92). However, Lesotho authorities have confirmed that since the launch of an online registration system on 15 December 2014, all information is freely accessible on the Registrar's website. The information kept on the register contains identification information on all legal owners of the company, including the name and contact details of all directors and shareholders (s. 21, Companies Regulations).

47. The Companies Act also provides for rules governing the incorporation and registration of companies with the Registrar (Part II, Companies Act). Any person(s) can make an application to the Registrar for the incorporation and registration of a company. This person is known as the "promoter" (s. 2). An application for incorporation may be submitted manually or electronically (s. 6) and must be accompanied by *(i)* a power of attorney if it is made by an agent or legal practitioner; and *(ii)* a certified copy of an identification document of a share subscriber and a director of the company. The application for incorporation must include contact details and passport information of at least two directors in the case of public companies, and at least one director for private companies. The contact details of all shareholders and directors must be submitted during the application (s. 5(5), 5(3)(b), Schedule Form 1, Form 8). In practice, a copy of the identification documents of the Directors and shareholders must be included with the registration application. When the Directors and shareholders are nationals from Lesotho, the OBFC checks that the identification provided (usually a license) is valid and has not expired. Foreigners are required to submit a copy of their passport which has to be certified by a Commissioner of oaths.

48. After receipt of completed application of incorporation, with all supporting documents including the articles of incorporation, the Registrar then registers the particulars of the company and issues a certificate of incorporation (s. 7(1)). Issuance of the certification of incorporation is confirmation that the company complies with all requirements of the Companies Act and that the company legally exists in Lesotho (s. 7).The articles of incorporation must prescribe rules and regulations for the management and operations of the company and adopt all or any of the model articles of incorporation developed by the Registrar under section 87(4). If no articles of incorporation are

registered, the model articles of information developed by the Registrar under section 87(4) shall apply. The articles of incorporation lodged for registration must also be signed by each promoter.

49. The Registrar may refuse to register a company based on factors such as registrations submitted with illegible documents, not in the prescribed form, with incomplete or improper information, etc. (s. 88(2)). The Registrar's refusal to register should not create a presumption as to the validity or invalidity of the document or the correctness or otherwise of the information contained in the document (s. 88(3)). Companies must submit true and accurate information with respect to any document required for purposes of the Companies Act. Any false statements made or authorised by a director, officer or employee of a company may result in conviction of the relevant persons to a fine up to LSL 500 000 (EUR 28 656) and/or imprisonment up to 20 years (s. 175). These measures also apply to persons who voted in favour of making such statements in a meeting (s. 175(3)).

50. Any changes in directorship in the company must be reported to the Registrar within 30 days of the change (s. 74(1)).Changes in directorship are reported to the OBFC through Form "9" in which the name of the new person being appointed and person ceased from appointment should be included. This form is used both for domestic and foreign (external) companies. Any additions or changes in shareholders must also be reported to the Registrar. Each time the company issues shares, the director of the company is required to lodge with the Registrar within 15 working days a form stating the number and the nominal amount of shares issued and the name and addresses of the persons to whom the shares have been issued (s. 20(3), Companies Act). In addition, the company is required to file with the Registrar a notice of transfer of shares within 30 working days of the transfer (s. 15(3), Companies Regulations). A company which fails to comply with the obligation to file notice of such transfer of shares is liable to payment of a late filing fee of LSL 5 (EUR 0.29) for each day of failure to file such form (Schedule 7, Companies Regulations).

51. The Registrar will also have information in the annual reports of all companies as companies are required to lodge its annual report with the Registrar annually within three months of the anniversary date of the incorporation of the company (s. 105(3)). Information that is required to be in the annual report includes information concerning changes in the business name and its subsidiaries, the address of the registered office, the agent for service, the place and address where company records are kept. The annual report will also have identity information on the directors, such as their names and addresses and of those who have ceased to hold office since the previous annual report, and the total remuneration and value of other benefits received by the directors and former directors during the financial year (s. 105(1)).

Failure to submit the regular annual report may result in removal of the company from the register of companies or a penalty as determined by the Minister (s. 108). During the review period there were no companies struck off from the Companies Registry and no sanctions were applied for failing to submit annual reports.

52. Companies that cease its business must inform the Registrar after all liquidation or dissolution processes are completed in accordance to the required procedures (Parts XVI, XVIII and XIX, Companies Act). Upon receiving the respective liquidation or dissolution reports and final accounts from the liquidator, the Registrar will endorse in the company's record in the register that the company is liquidated or dissolved (s. 152(2), 170(2), 174). Company accounts and records must be retained by the liquidator for a minimum of 10 years after the completion of the liquidation (s. 134(2)(d)).

53. The Registrar has the authority to remove a company from the register if the company fails to commence business within 12 months of incorporation, fails to submit an annual report, ceased its activities for 12 consecutive months, or if it has been absent at its registered address for 6 consecutive months (s. 87(5)). However, there was no oversight over the review period in this regard and consequently these measures were never applied in practice.

Information kept by the registrar of companies in practice

54. The OBFC is in charge of keeping the company registry in Lesotho. The OBFC is housed within the Registrar of Companies and staffed with nine officials: two deputy registrars of companies, two registry officers, two processing officers, two assistant processing officers and one compliance manager. The compliance manager is in charge of verifying that all obligations in the Companies Act are complied with.

55. The OBFC's authorities have reported that during the review period there was no oversight programme in place to monitor compliance of the obligations imposed on companies through the Companies Act. However, the OBFC further reported that in 2015 when moving the registry from a manual system to a desk-top system they realised they did not have updated director and shareholder information and so launched a "re-registration" compliance programme.

56. Re-registration was conducted by the compliance manager and an inspector and basically consisted in requiring all domestic and foreign (external) companies to update their information (including directors and shareholders) with OBFC. Companies who failed to re-register as at December 2015 were struck off from the registry and were given 15 days to apply for re-instatement. Companies that did not apply for reinstatement were struck off indefinitely from the Companies Registry. This compliance programme was

completed in March, with an end result of 17 591 (17 029 private companies, 504 public companies and 58 foreign (external) companies) struck-off companies out of a total of 29 030 companies altogether. The OBFC has reported that all information from struck-off companies will be kept indefinitely in their system, in the same manner as information on liquidated companies.

57. As at April 2016, a systematic compliance programme was put in place to regularly monitor the compliance with the obligations set forth in the Companies Act. Lesotho should monitor the implementation of this new oversight programme and exercise its enforcement powers as appropriate to ensure that ownership and identity information is available in practice.

Tax administration

58. The Lesotho Revenue Authority will generally not have updated ownership and identity information of companies as such information is not periodically included in the tax registration or filing of tax returns. However, Lesotho authorities indicate that in practice, LRA has access to updated ownership information through the OBFC's database. Therefore, all identity information and copies of the passports are available to the LRA. In addition, the LRA can verify ownership and identity information under the regular surveillance programme in place by the LRA, see A.2 *Availability of accounting records in practice*.

59. All taxpayers must file annual returns of income to the Commissioner General (s. 128) which must be accompanied with the company's financial statements such as a balance sheet, statement of income and expenses or other document that supported a return of income (s. 128(6)). Identity information on the legal owners of the company is not required to be included in such tax returns. Companies that make payments of Lesotho-source interest, dividends, royalties, management fees, rent or other income as specified by the Commissioner General must make a return of such payment to the Commissioner General within 28 days of the end of the year of assessment in which the payments were made. Such return must include the name, address, and, when appropriate, the taxpayer identification number (TIN) of each person to whom such payment was made, the amount paid (s. 130) and such additional information as the Commissioner General may require.

60. Failure to file a return as required by the Act is punishable per section 175 of the Act and the nominated officer for tax purposes of the company guilty of the offence is liable on conviction to a fine not exceeding LSL 5000 (EUR 287) or to imprisonment for a term not exceeding six months or both. Lesotho was unable to provide statistics as to how many times this fine was applied in practice.

Information held by companies

61. Legal obligations for companies to keep a share register are provided under section 29 of the Companies Act. All companies must maintain a share register with the names of all shareholders – current and within the last 10 years. If there are any transfers of shares, shareholders must inform the company and details of the share transfers must be entered on the share register within 15 days. Shareholders must be listed on the share register which will serve as evidence of their legal title to the shares. Falsely or deceitfully impersonating ownership of a share is an offence and is liable, upon conviction, to a fine of LSL10 000 (EUR 573) or imprisonment for a period of 3 years, or both. The Registrar of Companies has advised that this fine has never been applied in practice.

62. The share register must be kept in Lesotho. The director of the company is responsible for maintaining the share register and ensuring it is properly kept with updated information on share transfers. It should be kept at the registered office of the company unless – i) the maintenance of the register is carried out at another office of the company in Lesotho, whereby it may be kept at that office, or ii) the company arranges with some other person to maintain the register on behalf of the company, it may be kept at the office in Lesotho of that other person at which the work is done. For companies that engage an agent, the agent is responsible for maintaining the share register of the company. Any changes to the location where the share register is kept must be notified to the Registrar within 10 working days.

63. The Registrar has the authority to investigate companies if it suspects any fraud or irregularity (s. 87(9)). Any discovered criminal activity will be referred to the Director of Public Prosecutions and the Registrar's report can be used as evidence for prosecution (s. 87(10)). Any person that fails to provide any records as requested by the Registrar is liable to conviction to a fine of LSL 20 000 (EUR 1 147) or imprisonment for 3 years, or both (s. 87(12)).

64. During the review period Lesotho authorities did not have a regular oversight programme in place to monitor the compliance of the obligations set forth in the Companies Act. As at April 2016, a systematic compliance programme was put in place by OBFC to regularly monitor compliance of the obligations set forth in the Companies Act. Therefore, it is recommended that Lesotho monitors the implementation of this new oversight programme and exercises its enforcement powers as appropriate to ensure that ownership and identity information is available in practice.

Nominee identity information

65. In Lesotho, a nominee arrangement is carried out through the creation of a "voting trust" when one or more shareholders legally transfers its shares and the attached voting rights to a trustee (the nominee shareholder) (s.37, Companies Act). The availability of the identity information of the trustee (nominee) and shareholders it represents is ensured through legal requirements for the information to be submitted to the company, which is subsequently submitted to the Registrar. Lesotho's laws do not provide for the possibility of any other nominee arrangement other than through a "voting trust".

66. The provisions of the voting trust will be set out in an agreement signed by the shareholders and the trustee. Upon signing the agreement, the trustee is obligated to submit to the company's registered office a list of the names and addresses of shareholders who have an interest in the trust, together with the number and class of shares transferred to the trust. Once the shares subject to the trust are registered in the trustee's name, the voting trust is effective and is valid for a period not exceeding 10 years unless extended (s.37(3)). The company is responsible for verifying the legal status of the trustee (s.5(2), model Articles of Incorporation, Companies Regulation). Since the voting trust cannot be effective without the signed agreement by the shareholders who have an interest in the trust, any change in the ownership will be reflected in the signed agreement which must be delivered by the voting trustee to the company's registered office (s.37(5)).

67. The availability of ownership and identity information of such shareholders, whose shares are managed in a voting trust, is also ensured through AML obligations. Such trustees of voting trusts would be covered by the fact that they carry out the business of "safekeeping and administration of securities" which is a listed business under the Money Laundering and Proceeds of Crime Act (Schedule 1 (xv)). This qualifies them as an "accountable institution" under the Act and they are thereby subjected to the respective customer due diligence and know your customer obligations, which includes the requirement to keep all ownership and identity information of the shareholders for a minimum of five years from the end of the business relationship. Although Lesotho's laws only provide for nominee arrangements through a voting trust, if any other nominee arrangements were to exist, they would also be covered under the above-described AML obligations. Details of these obligations are described in a later section "Information kept by service providers and other persons".

68. Lesotho authorities have reported that no oversight has been conducted over the review period to verify compliance with the obligations imposed on service providers and other persons subject to AML rules. Therefore, it is recommended that Lesotho puts in place an oversight programme to ensure

compliance with the obligations to maintain ownership and identity information of voting trusts, and exercise its enforcement powers as appropriate to ensure that such information is available in practice.

Foreign companies ("external companies")

69. Foreign companies (or "external companies") are incorporated outside of Lesotho but have established a place of business within Lesotho. Similar to domestic companies, the legal obligations attached to external companies' registration with the Registrar ensures that all identifying information on the legal owners has to be maintained by the external company and provided to the Registrar at the time the company establishes a place of business in Lesotho and subsequently when there are any changes to its owners. As of March 2016, there are 56 external companies registered in Lesotho.

70. The rules for registration applicable to external companies are similar to that for domestic companies. External companies must apply for registration with the Registrar within ten days of establishing the place of business (s, 11(1), Companies Act).The application for registration must include the full names, nationality, residential addresses of the directors of the external company at the date of the application, the full address of the place of business of the external company in Lesotho, evidence of incorporation and a copy of the articles of incorporation of the company in English, full names and address of one or more persons resident in Lesotho who are authorised to accept service in Lesotho on behalf of the external company (s. 11(3)). There is no legal requirement in the law that such persons who accept service on behalf of external companies must be company service providers. Nonetheless, Lesotho authorities indicate that such persons who accept service typically include company service providers who are listed as an "accountable institution" under the Money Laundering and Proceeds of Crime Act (Schedule 1 (xxii)) and therefore also subjected to AML obligations to keep all ownership and identity information of the external company.

71. The obligations of the Registrar are the same for both domestic and external companies which includes the obligation to keep a register on all external companies. Upon receiving a completed application for registration, the Registrar shall immediately register it on the external register and issue a certificate of registration (s. 11(4)). If there are any changes to the articles of incorporation, directors or persons authorised to accept service in Lesotho of documents on behalf of the external company, the external company is to notify the Registrar within 20 days of the change or amendment (s. 12(2)). Identity information on all shareholders is one of the information items that the Registrar must ensure it keeps on the register (s. 21, Companies Regulations). Lesotho authorities have confirmed that legal obligations apply to external companies to keep identity information on its shareholders and

submit this information to the Registrar. This is based on the fact that "company" is defined as a body corporate "incorporated or registered" under the Companies Act (s. 2(1), Companies Act), and external companies are "registered" under the Companies Act. Lesotho authorities have also confirmed that these obligations do not differ as regards domestic or external companies. This includes the obligation to keep a share register and report any changes of its shareholders to the Registrar (s. 29, Companies Act and s. 15, Companies Regulations).

72. In practice, registration of foreign (external) companies is done in the same way as for domestic companies, see A.1.1 above *Types of companies*. However, external companies used a template registration form which did not have a specific field requesting ownership information (Schedule, Form 3, Companies Act) and the extent to which this information was available in practice was unknown. Foreign (external) companies are now registering with the same form used by domestic companies (Form 3) which contains ownership and identity information of the shareholders and requires that certified copies of the passport or identity document be attached.

73. If an external company intends to cease its business in Lesotho, it must within three months after giving public notice, notify the Registrar of its last date of business and the Registrar will remove the external company from the external register (s. 154). Lesotho authorities indicate that similar to the requirements in respect of domestic companies, accounts and records of the external company must be retained by the liquidator for a minimum of 10 years after the completion of the liquidation (s. 134(2)(d)).

74. External companies that have their management and control or undertake the majority of its operations in Lesotho are considered resident for tax purposes in Lesotho (s. 6(1), Income Tax Act). In addition, a branch of a non-resident company is treated as a separate person as if it is a resident company in Lesotho (s. 6(2)). All tax residents must file tax returns (s. 128) but as discussed earlier, tax returns by companies do not include all ownership and identity information and therefore are not relied on for EOI purposes.

75. As in the case of domestic companies, there was no oversight programme in place to monitor compliance of the obligations imposed on foreign (external) companies through the Companies Act during the review period. However, external companies were included within the re-registration compliance programme and will continue to be monitored through the new systematic compliance programme, see above *Information kept by public authorities – Registrar of companies*. It is recommended that Lesotho monitors the implementation of this new oversight programme and exercises its enforcement powers as appropriate to ensure that ownership and identity information for external companies is available in practice.

Information held by service providers and other persons

76. The Money Laundering and Proceeds of Crime Act of 2008 ("MLPC Act") which regulates AML rules in Lesotho requires persons providing services to a company to identify the owners of such company (s. 16). The MLPC Act defines "accountable institutions" in section 2 read with Schedule 1 as a person or institution including branches, associates or subsidiaries and employed or contracted persons outside such person or institution. These will include legal practitioners, accountants and financial institutions, as well as any person who carries on a business listed in the Act. For EOI purposes relating to companies, such other persons who may be relevant would include those carrying on a business of a company service provider (Schedule 1(c)(xxii)).

77. Under the MLPC Act, an accountable institution must, when establishing a business relationship, obtain information on the purpose and nature of the business relationship and, if the transaction is conducted by a natural person, adequately identify and verify his or her identity including information relating to the individual's name, address and occupation and the national identity card or passport or other applicable official identifying document (s. 16(1)). In the case of a transaction conducted by a legal entity, the accountable institution should adequately identify and verify its legal existence and structure, including information relating to the customer's name, legal status, address and directors and the principal owners and beneficiaries and control structure of the entity. In addition the accountable institution should establish the provisions regulating the power to bind the entity and verify that any person purporting to act on behalf of the customer is so authorised, and identify those persons (s. 16(1)).In the context of companies, Lesotho authorities advise that these AML rules are applied to include the obligation of company service providers to keep all ownership information of the company, including identity information of all members and shareholders.

78. The AML Guidelines further specify that in the case where a business relationship is conducted through an account, the accountable institution must obtain and verify the particulars of the identity of the customer or client at the time the banking of deposit account is opened. In cases where the business relationship is conducted on a one-off basis, a deposit taking accountable institution must obtain and verify the particulars of the identity of the customer or client at the time the transaction occurs, unless the deposit to, or by, the customer or client is less than LSL 20 000 (EUR 1 147).

79. The AML Guidelines state that where verification of the customer's or client's identity is satisfactorily completed, further verification is not necessary when the customer or client subsequently undertakes transactions as long as regular contact with the customer or client is maintained (s12(1)). Nonetheless, the AML Guidelines specify that an accountable institution must

monitor its customers or clients and their transactions on an on-going basis and observe the collection and verification of additional KYC information in relation to on-going customer due diligence (s. 16(1)). Where evidence of a person's identity is obtained in accordance with section 16 of the MLPC Act, a record that indicates the nature of the evidence obtained, and which comprises either a copy of the evidence or such information as would enable a copy of it to be obtained must be maintained by the accountable institution (s. 17(1)).

80. The obligation to maintain records is further described in the AML Guidelines where it is stated that the accountable institution must keep and maintain records of its customers or clients' business transactions that contain daily records of transactions, receipts, paying-in books, customer or client correspondence and cheques. Such records must be kept for a minimum of five years from when the business transaction is conducted (s. 17(1)). In addition, the AML Guidelines stipulate that an accountable institution should ensure that documents used to verify the identity of the customer or client and documents or information used to verify the identity of the beneficial owners are kept (s. 17(3)(c)). The records should also include records of on-going monitoring, documents or information on correspondent banking relationships and documentation on reliance on third parties, among other things (s. 17(3)). Such records should be kept by the accountable institution for a period of at least five years from the date the relevant business or transaction was completed, or termination of business relationship, whichever is the later (MLPC Act s. 17(4)).

81. An accountable institution which fails to comply with any AML requirements would be considered to have committed an offence, and is liable on conviction to a fine of not less than LSL 250 000 (EUR 14 326) (s. 26(3)). In the case of a natural person who fails to comply with any AML requirements would also be considered to have committed an offence and is liable to imprisonment for a period not exceeding 10 years, or a fine of not less than LSL 50 000 (EUR 2 865) or both. In addition or in the alternative to the fine mentioned above, the Court may order suspension or revocation of a business license (s. 26(4)). General penalties for non-compliance with the provisions of the Act may also apply where such persons are liable to a fine up to LSL 10 000 (EUR 573) or imprisonment for a period up to 30 months (s. 113).

Information held by service providers and other persons in practice

82. AML requirements are overseen by Lesotho's FIU. The FIU was created in 2010 after Lesotho underwent the Mutual Evaluation on Anti-Money Laundering and Combating the Financing of Terrorism conducted by the ESAAMLG. It has one Director and five Departments as follows: monitoring, legal and information services, compliance, information technology, and finance and administration.

83. The FIU has reported that the compliance department is very new and in the process of recruiting more staff. They did not conduct any surveillance of AML obligations during the review period and have only started with a programme to raise awareness among the accountable institutions. As at April 2016, there were 56 accountable institutions as follows:

Type of accountable institution	Number of institutions
Banks	4
Mobile money services	2
Accountants	4
Money lenders	13
Co-operative	1
Casinos and gambling houses	2
Insurance and insurance brokers	17
Money transmission services	1
Estates agencies	5
Legal practitioners	3
Foreign Exchange	3
Asset management	1

84. The FIU has informed that the initial work of the compliance department focused on raising awareness of AML obligations among accountable institutions. In November 2015 they engaged in the actual surveillance of the AML obligations, which consists on reviewing all AML policies the institutions must follow in accordance to the MLPC Act, including KYC and CDD obligations. As of August 2016, one bank was assessed. There were minor issues on non-compliance found during the assessment but none of which attracted a penalty. As a result of this assessment, the bank submitted a remedial action plan to address the recommendations given by the FIU. This means that during the review period, no oversight was conducted to verify compliance with the obligations imposed on service providers and other persons subject to AML rules. Further, none of the penalties contained in the MLPC for accountable institutions that fail to comply with AML obligations have been applied. It is recommended that Lesotho puts in place an oversight programme to ensure compliance with the obligations to maintain ownership information kept by service providers, particularly that of voting trusts, and exercise its enforcement powers as appropriate to ensure that such information is available in practice.

Conclusion

85. In principle, the legal and regulatory framework in Lesotho should ensure that ownership information regarding domestic and foreign (external) companies is available. The Companies Act requires all companies to provide identity information on all shareholders and directors upon registration with the Registrar of Companies, keep a share register and report any subsequent changes in directors or shareholders. Nominee ownership through voting trusts by trustees is covered by AML obligations and trustees must retain ownership and identity information of the shareholders they represent. Identification of the nominee and its shareholders, as well as the fact that the shares are held on behalf of another person must be entered in the register of shareholders held by the companies and where any update is to be reported to the Registrar of Companies. The obligations under the commercial and AML laws are in principle sufficient to ensure that ownership information on all companies in Lesotho is available in all cases, with exception to the cases of public companies that have issued share warrants to bearer as further analysed in section A.1.2 below.

86. However, during the review period there was no regular oversight programme in place to monitor compliance of AML obligations. Lesotho is recommended to put in place an oversight programme to ensure compliance with the obligations to maintain ownership information kept by service providers, particularly for voting trusts, and exercise its enforcement powers as appropriate to ensure that such information is available in practice. Lesotho authorities have reported that during the review period there was not a regular oversight programme in place to monitor compliance with the obligations contained in the Companies Act either. However, towards the end of 2015, a re-registration compliance programme was put in place requiring all domestic and external companies to re-register and update all the corporate information, including that of directors and shareholders, see *A.1.1 Companies*. In 2016, a new regular oversight programme was put in place to continue monitoring these obligations. Lesotho should monitor the implementation of this new oversight programme and exercise its enforcement powers as appropriate to ensure that ownership and identity information is available in practice.

87. During the review period Lesotho received one request regarding identity and ownership information of companies. The Lesotho competent authority was able to provide the requested ownership information.

Bearer shares *(ToR A.1.2)*

88. There is no legislation in Lesotho regarding bearer shares. The issuance of bearer shares is effectively impeded through registration requirements under the Companies Act. As discussed in section A.1.1, a person can

only be legally entitled to the rights associated with the shares of a company when that person's name is entered in the company's share register (s. 29). It is therefore not possible to own shares in a company without having your name entered in the share register.

89. However, upon closer inspection of the model articles of incorporation provided in the Companies Regulation which public companies may adopt, it appears that "share warrants to bearer" may be issued by a public company in Lesotho if allowed under the company's articles of incorporation (s. 9, Companies Regulation Schedule 3).If allowed, such share warrants may be issued with respect of fully paid shares and entitles the bearer to the shares specified. A share represented by a share warrant may be transferred by delivery of the warrant representing it. Bearers of share warrants are entitled to the same rights and privileges as they would if their names had been included in the register as holders of the shares represented by their warrants. Bearers are also entitled to attend and vote at the general meetings, receive payments of dividends and surrender their warrants so as to hold their shares in certificated or uncertificated form (s. 10, Companies Regulation Schedule 3). Lesotho authorities have indicated that shares in "uncertificated form" refer to shares that are credited to the account of a shareholder without the physical issuance of a certificate. The name of the shareholder is entered in the register and any transfer of shares is recorded by updating the identity information of the particular shareholder in the register.

90. These provisions for share warrants, if provided in the public company's articles of incorporation, do not appear to impose any requirements for the company to retain any ownership information of share warrants to bearer. However, when read with the definition of "shareholders" under the Companies Act, it may appear that share warrants to bearer are subjected to the same treatment as shareholders as regards to companies' obligation to keep updated identity information of all holders of shares on its share register (s. 29, Companies Act), and update the Registrar on any transfers of shares, i.e. changes in the holder of shares (s. 15(3), Companies Regulation). These obligations were also described in the previous section on companies which also ensures the availability of ownership information in line with the international standard. A shareholder refers to a person who is the "holder" of a share (s. 2, Companies Act), and in the case for a public company that issues share warrants, the "holder" includes the person "in possession of that warrant" (s. 1, Companies Regulation Schedule 3). In addition, since bearer of share warrants are also entitled to the same rights as a shareholder, such as attending and voting at general meetings and receiving dividends, it would also be reasonably expected that the company should have identification information on holders of share warrants.

91. The rules in the Companies Act, when read together, appear to provide for public companies to keep ownership information in respect of all share warrants to bearer, and not be inconsistent with the requirement under the Companies Act to record all ownership information of shares (s. 29), and that a person can only be legally entitled to the rights of shares if the person's name is entered in the share register (s. 29).

92. Lesotho authorities have confirmed that the above interpretation of the rules in the Companies Act and the Companies Regulations is applied in Lesotho, and these rules allow the availability of identification information of the holders of share warrants. In addition, Lesotho authorities have advised that the policy is that permission must be sought from the Minister responsible for trade and industry before any public company can issue share warrants. It is however unclear what the criteria for granting the permission are. Notwithstanding, Lesotho authorities have confirmed that share warrants have never been issued as none of these public companies have sought the relevant permission. This is likely due to the small size and nature of companies that operate in Lesotho. As of March 2016, the total number of public companies that may issue share warrants is 628, which represents 2.25% of all companies in Lesotho.

93. Lesotho authorities reported that during the review period there were no cases of public companies requesting permission from the MTICM to issue share warrants to bearer. However, no specific investigation was conducted to find out whether any of the public companies registered in Lesotho had issued share warrants to bearer in the past. Ownership of companies was also verified through the re-registration programme, see A.1.1 *Information kept by the registrar of companies in practice*, and no share warrants to bearer were encountered in the course of this programme. Further, the Registrar of Companies considers that the nominal ownership principle prevails as information on shareholders, as well as subsequent changes in ownership, needs to be provided and updated annually with the Registrar of Companies. In addition, the Lesotho Revenue Authorities have never encountered share warrants to bearer in the course of their tax audits.

94. Lesotho did not receive any request for information regarding ownership of share warrants to bearer during the review period. Nevertheless, the situation remains that 628 public companies registered in Lesotho could issue share warrants to bearer and the mechanisms in place to require ownership information pertaining to the issuance of such warrants may be insufficient.

Conclusion

95. The mechanisms laid out in the Companies Act should impede the issuance of bearer shares despite there being no explicit prohibition on bearer

shares. The existing rules under these laws appear to be sufficient to ensure that ownership information of all shares are available since details of any share transfer must be recorded and reported, and that persons can only claim their legal title to the shares if they are listed on the share register. These rules appear to allow for the availability of identification information of all holders of share warrants. Lesotho authorities have also confirmed that no share warrants have ever been issued, as there has been no application by any public company to seek the necessary permission from the Minister to do so. The number of public companies that may issue share warrants is 628, representing 2.25% of all companies in Lesotho. Notwithstanding, as there are also no express provisions in the laws requiring ownership information to be retained specifically in respect of all share warrants to bearer, there remains some uncertainty as to whether the mechanisms are sufficiently robust to ensure the availability of information identifying all holders of share warrants to bearer. Given that share warrants to bearer is expressly allowed for under Lesotho's laws, and the situation remains that 628 public companies registered in Lesotho could issue share warrants to bearer it is recommended that Lesotho should take necessary measures to ensure that robust mechanisms are in place to identify the owners of share warrants to bearer or eliminate companies' ability to issue such share warrants.

Partnerships (ToR A.1.3)

96. Partnerships in Lesotho are governed under the Partnership Proclamation No. 78 of 1957, which provides for two types of partnerships:

- A **partnership** is defined as any legal relationship between any two or more persons, but not exceeding 20 persons, who carry on, or intend to carry on, any lawful business or undertaking to which each person contributes something, with the object of making a profit and of sharing it between them (s. 1). There are currently 236 partnerships registered with the Lesotho Revenue Authority in Lesotho.
- A **limited partnership** must bear all the requirements of a partnership as defined but it is distinct in that it consists of two classes of partners, general partners, who are jointly and severally liable for the debts of the partnership and who have the authority to transact on behalf of the partnership, and one or more special partners who contribute specific sums of money and whose liability for the debts of the partnership is generally limited to their contributions and have no authority to transact on behalf of the partnership (s. 11 and 12).There are currently no limited partnerships registered in Lesotho.

Information kept by public authorities

Information provided to the Registrar of Deeds

97. Both a partnership and limited partnership obtains legal personality upon registration of their deed of partnership with the Registrar of Deeds (s. 2(1), Partnership Proclamation). All partners are to sign the deed of partnership that records all terms of the partnership. The deed is prepared by a legal practitioner and must be signed by the partners before a notary or an administrative officer, and registered with the Registrar within 60 days. The Registrar of Deeds will examine the deed to verify it complies fully with the legal requirements before proceeding with registration.

98. The partnership deed for both partnerships and limited partnerships must include all identification information on all partners. This includes the full names, residential addresses, amount of capital or assets brought into the partnership by every partner, duties and degree of participation of each partner in the business of the partnership, proportions for sharing of profits and losses, etc. (s. 5(1)). For limited partnerships that also consist of special partners, the deed must also include identification information on the special partners and the amount of capital brought into the partnership by each of the special partner (s. 13). Every partner must include upon registration a copy of their identification document certified by a commissioner of oaths.

99. Any changes to information in the partnership deed, including dissolution of the partnership, would need to be recorded in the form of a deed that will again be signed by all partners before a notary or an administrative officer. The revised deed must be registered with the Registrar within 60 days (s. 6(1)).

100. The Registrar is responsible for reviewing the information submitted in the partnership deed and may decline to register any partnership if it does not comply with the requirements of the Partnerships Proclamation or any other law relating to registration of deeds (s. 10(1)(a)). Unregistered partnerships will have no legal status and cannot enforce any rights arising out of any contract made or entered on behalf of any unregistered partnership (s. 28). There are no other sanctions indicated in the law, such as for partnerships that fail to submit any changes to its partnership deed.

101. Officials from the Registrar of Deeds have reported that their registration system is done manually in a ledger. There are no compliance or inspections sections within the Registrar of Deeds and consequently, no monitoring on partnerships is conducted after registration is completed. On application of fines, see A.1.6 *Enforcement provisions to ensure availability of information.*

102. The Registrar of Deeds has reported that the LRA has never requested from them information on partnerships. If the LRA is to request information on a partnership, they should be able to retrieve this information within one day. However, the information contained within the registration ledger kept by the Registrar of Deeds seems to be unreliable, for example, Registrar of Deeds has reported that as of April 2016 they have 22 partnerships registered while LRA reports to have 236.

Information provided to the tax administration

103. All partnerships with at least one resident partner are considered resident for tax purposes in Lesotho and non-resident partnerships receiving chargeable income in Lesotho are subject to tax (s. 7, Income Tax Act). A partnership is considered resident for tax purposes if one or all partners of the partnership were resident in Lesotho during the year of assessment (s. 7, ITA). In the case of non-resident partnerships, income of the partnership is taxed at the level of the partners, i.e. the non-resident partnership is considered tax transparent (s. 4(3)).

104. A partnership resident and carrying on business in Lesotho is obliged to file an annual return of income to the Commissioner General (s. 128, Income Tax Act). A partnership is a resident partnership for a year of assessment if at any time during that year a partner was a resident of Lesotho (s. 7, Income Tax Act). Lesotho authorities have also confirmed that the laws are interpreted to require non-resident (foreign) partnerships operating in Lesotho to file such returns through its nominated officer. Although partners rather than the partnership are taxed, the partnership is required to file a return for the income of the partnership (s. 75(1)). All partnerships must file a tax return through its nominated officer who must be a resident in Lesotho (s. 128 and s. 211(2)). The tax return must be accompanied with the partnership's financial statements such as a balance sheet, statement of income and expenses or other document that supported a return of income (s. 128(6)). Identity information on all partners will be included in the tax return since it must list all partners of the partnership and their profit allocation (Income Tax Return Form).

Information provided to the tax administration in practice

105. The income tax return form contains a specific section in which the information of the partners in a partnership must be included. This information includes: name of the partner, tax identification number, postal address, if the partner is resident or not and the percentage of interest the partner holds in the partnership.

106. In addition to the obligation on the partnership to file annual tax returns, every partnership that makes payments of Lesotho-source interests, dividends, royalties, management fees, rent, or other income as specified by the Commissioner must make a return of such payment to the Commissioner General within 28 days of the end of the year of assessment in which the payments were made, setting out, amongst other things, the name, address and where appropriate, the tax identification number of each person to whom such payments were made (s. 130).

107. The nominated officer of any partnership who fails to file a return or document as required under the Income Tax Act is guilty of an offence and liable on conviction to a fine not exceeding LSL 5 000 (EUR 286) or to imprisonment for a term not exceeding six months, or both (s. 175(1)). Lesotho was unable to produce statistics over the review period for sanctions imposed on partnerships for failure to file annual tax returns during the review period.

108. Compliance levels for partnerships filing annual tax returns were as follows during the review period:

Year	Compliance rate
2013	19%
2014	25%
2015	26%

Information held by the partners and service providers

109. All identity information is included in the partnership deed, which also has to be signed before the notary or administrative officer where changes occur. The deed is produced in duplicate where one remains with the Registrar and the others with the partnership. Section 8 of the Partnership Proclamation provides that the deed of partnership if recorded and expressed in any language other than English or Sesotho will have to be translated to either of the languages.

110. Section 16 of the MLPC Act 2008 requires all accountable institutions, including lawyers, accountants, financial institutions and other persons who carry on a host of such services as financial services, insurance services, gaming and gambling services, custody and safekeeping services etc. to, when establishing any business relationship or carrying out any business transaction, obtain full information about the nature and purpose of such relationship or transaction. If the relationship or transaction is with a legal entity, an accountable institution is required to adequately identify and verify its legal existence and structure, including information relating to customer's name, legal status, address and directors (presumably partners as well),

the principal owners and beneficiaries and control structure and provisions relating to the power to bind the entity and to verify that any such person purporting to act on behalf of the customer is authorised and identify those persons. In the context of partnerships, Lesotho authorities advise that these AML rules are applied to include the obligation of company service providers to keep all identity information of all partners of the partnership. Guidelines 5 – 9 of the Anti-Money Laundering Guidelines and the KYC Guidelines of 2007 also require financial institutions to establish and record as much information as possible about identities of all persons concerned with ownership of a legal entity, including partnerships. Lesotho authorities have not applied any enforcement mechanisms to ensure compliance of AML obligations in practice (see A.1 *Information held by service providers and other persons in practice*).

111. All information on the partnerships must be kept in Lesotho. Partnerships that carry on business or derive income in Lesotho should have a nominated officer for tax purposes and where one of the partners is a resident, that partner should be the nominated officer (s. 211). This is consistent with the requirement for documents to be kept in Lesotho where such documents can be obtained from the nominated officer in Lesotho (s. 169, Income Tax Act).

Conclusion

112. The legal and regulatory framework ensures that ownership information regarding all partnerships is available. All partnerships must be registered in Lesotho to have legal effect. Partnerships are required to submit information on all their partners to the Registrar of Deeds and report any subsequent changes. Tax laws require all partnerships, including foreign partnerships, to include the identity information on all partners of the partnership and their profit allocation when filing tax returns. Compliance levels of tax filing obligations for partnerships are low in Lesotho and do not ensure the availability in practice, of the information of all partners in a partnership. The CDD and KYC obligations under AML laws also further ensure the availability of ownership information for partnerships where service providers are engaged. In practice, it is not possible to rely on information kept by the service providers since the Lesotho authorities have not applied any enforcement mechanisms to ensure compliance with AML obligations.

113. In the three year review period, Lesotho has not received any EOI requests for information relating to partners in a partnership. Considering that minimum oversight was exercised by the Registrar of Deeds and by the LRA through the filing of annual tax returns, it is unclear whether information on partners of a partnership would be available in Lesotho if requested by a treaty partner. Therefore, it is recommended that Lesotho puts in

place an oversight programme to ensure compliance with the obligations to maintain ownership and identity information of partnerships, and exercise enforcement powers as appropriate to ensure that such information is available in practice.

Trusts (ToR A.1.4)

114. There is no statutory law dealing with the creation, administration, monitoring and regulation of trusts in Lesotho. Notwithstanding, trusts can be created in Lesotho under common law, where there is a general duty on trustees to maintain proper records of the trust property and to have knowledge of all documents pertaining to the formation and management of a trust. These documents typically include the identity of settlors, beneficiaries and other trustees. Upon registration with the Registrar of Deeds, a copy of the identification document of the parties to the trust, duly certified by a commissioner of oaths, needs to be included. This is similar to and enunciated in the South African law, which Lesotho references given the high persuasive value that South African judicial decisions have in Lesotho. Lesotho authorities have advised that it can be interpreted that trusts can be created in Lesotho under Lesotho's common law, guided by the principles and rules under the Friendly Societies Act of 1882. As of March 2016 there are 40 trusts registered with the Registrar of Deeds and 52 registered with the LRA

115. Generally, the criteria for the creation of a trust are similar to the English common law, namely a trust is created where assets are transferred by a person (the settlor) to a trustee for the benefit of another person. Lesotho laws do not prohibit a resident of Lesotho from acting as a trustee or otherwise in a fiduciary capacity in relation to a trust formed under foreign law. Likewise, Lesotho laws also do not prohibit a resident of Lesotho from administering a trust governed under foreign law. Apart from the extent that the Friendly Societies Act is referenced, there are no clear rules for the registering of trusts with any authority in Lesotho.

116. The laws examined to determine if the legal and regulatory framework of Lesotho ensures the availability of all identity information of the trustee, settlor and beneficiary of all trusts in Lesotho are the Friendly Societies Act, Income Tax Act and the AML laws and guidelines.

Friendly Societies Act

117. When read with the Friendly Societies Act, trusts are to appoint one or more persons to be a trustee and a copy of the resolution is to be deposited with the Registrar of Deeds (s. 3). Lesotho authorities apply common law principles where the settlor has unfettered discretion as to who to appoint as a trustee. In this regard, Lesotho authorities reference the South African case of *Land and*

Agricultural Bank of South Africa v Parker 2005 (2) SA 77 (SCA), Cameron JA stated that "…Who the trustees are, their number, how they are appointed, and under what circumstance they have power to bind the trust estate are matters defined in the trust deed, which is the trust's constitutive charter. Outside its provisions the trust estate can not be bound" (on Page 10 Para 83H).

118. The Friendly Societies Act also contains provisions on the general requirements for the keeping of audited accounts of the society or in this case, the trust (s. 10(5)). Annual returns must also be submitted to the Registrar of Deeds and include general financial statements on the use of funds and the annual report of the society (or trust). The Registrar of Deeds has reported that in practice trusts have never submitted these annual returns and fines have never been applied on account of not submitting such returns.

119. There are no explicit requirements under the Friendly Societies Act for the trust to keep or report any identity information on all parties to the society, or in the case of a trust – the settlor, trustee and beneficiary. Lesotho authorities have indicated that the policy adhered to by trusts in Lesotho is that a trust deed is created by the lawyer nominated by the person(s) who wish to start a trust. The deed is thereafter submitted to the Ministry of Local Government for registration into the Deeds Registry. Foreign trusts also have to submit the trust deed to the Deeds Registry if it wishes to operate in Lesotho. While there is no requirement that the trusts must submit all identity information on all parties to the trust, the information may be in the trust deed as is typically the case for most trusts established under common law. Since trusts are not explicitly provided for under the Friendly Societies Act, it is also unclear how any of the obligations in this Act can be enforced for trusts in practice. In practice, the provisions contained in the Friendly Societies Act are not being enforced in respect of trusts. Notwithstanding the above, an obligation to identify the trustee, settlor and beneficiary of trusts are provided under the Income Tax Act and the AML laws and guidelines, as further described below.

Income Tax Act

Types of trusts

120. For tax purposes, a trust is a separate taxable entity and it includes the estate of a deceased person. A "trustee" is defined under the Income Tax Act (s. 3(1)) as:

i. an executor, administrator, tutor, or curator; and

ii. a liquidator or judicial manager; and

iii. a person having or taking on the administration or control of property subject to a trust;

iv. a person acting in a fiduciary capacity; and

v. a person having the possession, control, or management of the property of a person under a legal disability.

121. A trust as defined under the Income Tax Act does not include a "grantor trust" or a "qualified beneficiary trust" (s. 2(1), Income Tax Act).

- A "grantor trust" is a trust in which the grantor (or settlor) has (either in whole or in part) *(a)* the power to revoke or alter the trust so as to acquire a beneficial interest in the corpus or income or *(b)* a reversionary interest in either the corpus or income.
- A "qualified beneficiary trust" is a trust in which a person has a power solely exercisable by that person to vest the corpus or income in that person or a trust whose sole beneficiary is an individual or an individual's estate or appointees.

122. A grantor trust or a qualified beneficiary trust is not treated as a separate taxable entity from the grantor or beneficiary, respectively. Income from a grantor trust is reported directly on the grantor's tax return, and income from a qualified beneficiary trust is reported directly on the beneficiary's return.

123. The Income Tax Act also provides for unit trusts. Unit trusts refer to that under the Lesotho Unit Trust Act 2003, which are medium to long-term collective investment schemes managed by STANLIB Lesotho (Pty) Ltd, a licensed financial services provider regulated by the Central Bank of Lesotho under the Collective Investment Schemes Regulations 2001. A unit trust is exempt from all taxes under the Income Tax Act. However, when filing their tax returns, the unit holders must include in income any returns realised from the unit trust, except if there are bonus units, which in such cases the sale of such bonus shall be deemed as equivalent to dividends and may be subjected to tax (s. 83C). Despite the limited identity information available as part of tax obligations, Lesotho authorities have confirmed that the STANLIB Lesotho (Pty) Ltd would, as a licensed financial services provider, be subjected to AML obligations to maintain all information of its customers, which in respect of the Lesotho Unit Trust, would include identity information on all unit holders. However, Lesotho authorities have not applied any enforcement mechanisms to ensure compliance of AML obligations in practice (see A.1 *Information held by service providers and other persons in practice*).

Information provided to the tax authorities

124. Apart from the exceptions for a grantor trust, qualified beneficiary trust and a unit trust, all other trusts that "carries on business in Lesotho or derives Lesotho-source income" (s. 211(1)) must have a nominated officer for

tax purposes who is responsible for any tax obligation imposed on the trust, including the filing of tax returns (s. 211(6)).This is the same obligation for companies and partnerships as described in A.1.1 and A.1.3. For trusts with a resident trustee, the nominated officer must be the resident trustee (s. 211(2)). Since every entity must have a nominated officer for tax purposes, it may be inferred that trusts without a resident trustee but that "carries on a business in Lesotho or derives Lesotho-source income" must appoint a nominated officer. Lesotho authorities also interpret that for a trust, the nominated officer must be a person resident in Lesotho. This would be consistent with the requirements for other entities that the nominated officer must be a resident person (s. 211), and that all records for tax purposes are to be maintained in Lesotho (s. 169), for which this obligation would presumably be imposed on the nominated officer. All trusts must appoint the nominated officer in the first year of assessment and notify the Commissioner General, failing which the Commissioner General will specify the person to be the nominated officer (s. 211(3) and (4)). Trusts must also notify the Commissioner General of any changes to their nominated officers (s. 211(5)).

125. All ordinary trusts that have taxable income are required to file a tax return annually to the LRA (s. 81(7)). Lesotho authorities confirm that the annual filing obligation applies regardless whether income or loss has been made. Trust income or loss is calculated as if the trust were a resident individual taxpayer, minus personal deductions and credits. Trust income is taxed in the hands of trustees (s. 83) where the trustee is liable for income tax on the chargeable trust income. The chargeable trust income includes Lesotho-source income and foreign-source income, and is calculated by subtracting the amount included in the gross income of any beneficiary (s. 83(2)). The foreign-source income that is included refers to when the settlor is resident at the time of making a transfer to the trustee; or is a resident in the year of assessment in question; or where a resident person may ultimately benefit from the income (s. 83(1)), and subtracting the gross income of any beneficiary (s. 83(2)). Beneficiaries are taxable on their share of trust income to which they are presently entitled (s. 82) and are therefore responsible in all instances for filing their own income tax returns. Non-resident beneficiaries are only taxed on Lesotho-source income of the trust to which the beneficiary is presently entitled (s. 82(2)). The tax return should be in a form prescribed by the Commissioner General and will contain information on income, expenditure and details of the nominated officer who is responsible for accurately assessing the tax payable.

126. The Income Tax Act is not explicit as to whether the tax return has to indicate the identity information on the settlor, trustee and beneficiary of each trust. Notwithstanding, in view of the tax treatment of trusts, identity information of the trustees would be included in the returns to determine the taxable income since trusts are taxed at the trustee level. As trustees would

have to prove the residence status of the settlor to determine its taxable income, it should follow that identity information of the settlor would also have to be included in the returns. The identity information on beneficiaries would also be known in some cases since beneficiaries are responsible for filing their own income tax returns on their share of trust income. In addition, nominated officers are also obligated to notify the Commissioner General of the identity of any non-resident beneficiaries (s. 211(6)).

127. As the obligations under the Income Tax Act only apply where the trust income is taxable, there may still be gaps as regards the availability of ownership information of trusts that have a nexus to Lesotho (i.e. established in Lesotho under common law, has a resident trustee in Lesotho or administered in Lesotho). Identity information may not be available for trustees and settlors of a trust, which only receives foreign-source income and where the settlor is not a resident. Such trust income would not be liable to tax and the trustee of such a trust, even if there is a resident trustee, would not be required to register or file a tax return. There may also be a gap in the availability of identity information of beneficiaries who are *(i)* resident in Lesotho but are not entitled to any of the trust income for the year;*(ii)* resident in Lesotho and entitled to trust income which is foreign-sourced and where the settlor is non-resident; and *(iii)* non-resident in Lesotho but whose entitled share of the trust income is foreign-sourced. Notwithstanding, Lesotho authorities confirm that AML rules mitigate these gaps as analysed in the next section.

AML rules

128. AML rules do not specifically provide for trustees but contain obligations for all financial institutions, and other accountable persons who may act as professional trustees including legal practitioners, accountants and company service providers, to maintain ownership information of all parties to the trust. Lesotho authorities indicate that the provision of trustee services by any other person or entity appears to be very rare as the use of trusts is not prevalent in Lesotho and any trusts set up are usually family trusts established through a lawyer by parents for their children. Entities and persons covered by AML rules are obligated to determine whether a customer is acting on behalf of another person as a trustee, nominee or any other intermediary (Financial Institutions (KYC) Guidelines 2007). "Customer" is also defined as beneficial owners of transactions conducted by professional intermediaries including legal practitioners, accountants and company service providers. In doing so, the financial institution must obtain identity information of such persons and should establish the nature of the relationship and arrangement in place. While opening an account for a trust, the financial institution must take reasonable precautions to identify trustees,

settlors of trusts, grantors, protectors, beneficial owners and signatories (Schedule 1, Guideline 9(4)).Where the account for the trust is opened by a professional intermediary, which may include legal practitioners, accountants or company service providers, the financial institution is also subjected to the same obligations to obtain all identity information on all parties to the trust (Schedule 1, Guideline 9(4)(1.2)). The general penalty prescribed in the Financial Institutions Act (s. 32) will apply for non-compliance and prescribes that a penalty not exceeding LSL 500 000 (EUR 28 650) will apply in a continuing offence and an additional daily penalty not exceeding LSL 5 000 (EUR 286), in contravention of any provision of the Act. These penalties were never applied during the review period.

129. The KYC procedures applicable to banks and other accountable institutions are described in the Money Laundering (Accountable Institutions) Guidelines, Legal Notice no. 55 of 2013 (the AML Guidelines). The AML Guidelines specify that an accountable institution, including legal practitioners, accountants and company service providers, should obtain and verify particulars of identity of trustees, nominees, or fiduciaries and the underlying beneficiary on whose behalf a business transaction is entered into, and establish the purpose of which the transaction is entered into (s. 6(4)(b)). In addition, a deposit taking accountable institution is obliged to obtain and verify the identity of a third party if the deposit is by, or on behalf of, a third party (s. 13).

130. The Financial Institutions Guidelines of 2007, Schedule 1, guideline 1(1.4) provides that while opening an account for a foundation, financial institution must take reasonable precautions to verify the identity of the founders, managers or directors and beneficial owners. Under section 17(4) of the MLPC Act, identify information must be retained for at least 5 years. It is not specified in the Act if the information is to be kept within Lesotho although Lesotho authorities have confirmed that this would be indicated in the respective industry-specific legislation.

Trust ownership information in practice

131. Lesotho authorities have reported that in principle, every trust should register with the Registrar of Deeds. However, there is no express legal provision requiring trusts to register. The Registrar of Deeds has informed that there are 40 trusts registered in Lesotho, while there are 52 registered with the LRA. Trusts that do register with the Registrar of Deeds should provide upon registration, a copy of the identification document of the parties to the trust, duly certified by a commissioner of oaths.

132. Trusts that conduct business in Lesotho need to obtain a business license from OBFC and register with the LRA. To obtain the business license,

trusts are required to fill in a form with OBFC and provide information on the parties to the trust (settlor, trustee and beneficiaries). Trusts are also required to identify the parties to the trust when registering with the LRA.

133. In addition, trusts file an annual tax return to the LRA through form S128-TE which needs to be signed by the nominated officer, who is also the resident trustee. Information on the nominated officer includes the full name and the taxpayer identification number. This form also requires filling the information of the trust beneficiaries. There is a specific section (part K) to indicate the name, taxpayer identification number, postal address and whether or not the beneficiary is a resident beneficiary. This section should include the information on all beneficiaries, disregarding whether or not they are entitle to trust income. Further, part H of the form requires that the allocation of shares of income or foreign tax paid to beneficiaries is also disclosed. The LRA monitors through the filing of the annual income tax returns that ownership and identity information is available for trusts. However, the LRA was unable to produce statistics on tax filing compliance of trusts during the review period, as well as statistics on penalties imposed for failure to file annual tax returns. Tax filing compliance reported for other type of entities was low, see *A.1.3 Partnerships*.

134. Information might not be available for trusts that are not subject to tax in Lesotho as they are not required to file annual income tax returns. In principle, ownership information for trusts that are not subject to tax in Lesotho should be available with the Registrar of Deeds or with a service provider. However, in practice, trusts do not always register with the Registrar of Deeds and although the obligations for services providers under the AML laws in principle ensure that this information is available, the FIU has reported that during the review period they did not conduct any oversight over AML obligations and it is therefore uncertain the extent to which this information is available in practice, see A.1.1 Information held by service providers and other persons.

Conclusion

135. The combination of common law, tax law and AML obligations ensure the availability of identity information on trustees, settlors and beneficiaries in respect of trusts created under Lesotho laws, administered in Lesotho, or in respect of a resident trustee of a foreign trust in Lesotho:

1. Common law imposes obligations on the trustee to maintain information on the trust beneficiaries and settlors. The common law places obligations on trustees to have full knowledge of all the trust documents, to act in the best interests of the beneficiaries and only distribute assets to the right persons. These obligations implicitly

require all trustees to identify all the beneficiaries of the trust since this is the only way the trustee can carry out his duties properly. If the trustees fail to meet their common law obligations, they are liable to being sued. However, it should also be noted that foreign trusts formed under non-common law jurisdictions may not adhere to common law obligations. Lesotho authorities have reported that in principle common law obligations are ensured through the registration of trusts with the Registrar of Deeds. However, since there is no express legal provision containing the obligation for trusts to register with the Registrar of Deeds, trusts not always register. Currently the Registrar of Deeds has 40 trusts registered while there are 52 trusts registered with the LRA.

2. Tax law ensures the availability of identity information on trustees, settlors and beneficiaries to the extent that the trust income is taxable in Lesotho. Identity information on non-resident beneficiaries must be reported to the tax authorities. However, identity information may not be available in respect of trustees and settlors of trusts that do not have taxable trust income and beneficiaries that do not have taxable trust income, and thus may not be required to report the identity information when filing tax returns. The LRA has advised that changes in ownership necessarily impact the tax obligations of the parties to the trust and therefore, updated information is available through the annual tax return filed by the trustee. However, this is not the case for those trusts which are not subject to tax in Lesotho. Furthermore, LRA was unable to produce statistics on tax filing compliance of trusts during the review period, as well as statistics on penalties imposed on trusts for failure to file annual tax returns. In addition, tax filing compliance reported for other type of entities was low, see *A.1.3 Partnerships*.

3. AML rules provide for obligations to keep the identity information on all parties to the trust where trusts are managed by professional trustees when they are legal practitioners, accountants and company service providers. Lesotho authorities have clarified that the use of trusts is not prevalent in Lesotho, it is rare to have trusts managed by any other entity or person or non-professional trustees and they are not aware of any that exist in Lesotho. In addition, obligations are also placed with financial institutions to keep identity information on all parties of trusts that open trust accounts. However, Lesotho authorities do not have regular oversight to monitor the compliance of AML obligations.

4. Although trusts may be loosely administered under the Friendly Societies Act, this legislation does not appear to include adequate

obligations to ensure the availability of identity information on the trustee, settlor and beneficiaries. In practice, the provisions contained in the Friendly Societies Act are not being enforced in respect of trusts.

136. It is also conceivable that a trust could be created under the laws of Lesotho, which has no other connection with Lesotho. In that event, there may be no information about the trust available in Lesotho. Lesotho authorities have reported that they have never encountered such a case in practice.

137. In practice, updated ownership and identity information of trusts subject to tax in Lesotho should be available with the LRA through the filing of annual tax returns. However, the LRA was unable to produce statistics on tax filing compliance of trusts during the review period, as well as statistics on penalties imposed on trusts for failure to file annual tax returns. In addition, tax filing compliance for other type of entities, such as partnerships, was low. For trusts that are not subject to tax in Lesotho, information should be available either with the Registrar of Deeds or with a service provider. Nonetheless, in practice, not all trusts register with the Registrar of Deeds. Further, Lesotho authorities do not regularly monitor the compliance of AML obligations and it is therefore uncertain the extent to which this information is available in practice. Lesotho should monitor the compliance of the legal obligations to maintain ownership and identity information for trusts, and exercise its enforcement powers as appropriate to ensure that such information is available in practice.

138. In the three year review period (1 July 2012-30 June 2015), Lesotho has not received any EOI requests for information relating to trusts.

Foundations *(ToR A.1.5)*

139. There is no specific law for the establishment of foundations in Lesotho and based on the features of the entities called "foundations" that exist in Lesotho, it may be concluded that these are not relevant for the work of the Global Forum.

140. Lesotho authorities have advised that most entities called "foundations" are established as non-profit making companies in Lesotho. All 67 non-profit making companies registered in Lesotho are called "foundations" and are therefore subjected to the same rules as companies which has been analysed under A.1.1. Other foundations not registered as non-profit making companies are registered under the Societies Act 20 of 1966.

141. According to Lesotho authorities, all entities called "foundations" in Lesotho pursue non-profit activities which are intended to be in the interest of the public such as to promote human health and education. Since the

foundations support a general cause and benefit general categories of people (e.g. youths, disadvantaged communities or orphans) there are no identifiable beneficiaries. Members of founders of the foundations do not receive any distribution nor benefit from the sale of the foundation's property or assets upon its dissolution. Instead, assets are handed over to another foundation of a similar cause or handed over to the State. Lesotho authorities have confirmed that while there is no legal requirement, this is the common practice adhered to. Foundations are also exempted from tax. All foundations must seek approval of its activities with the Registrar prior to its incorporation as a non-profit company. Lesotho authorities indicate this is an administrative requirement as there is no licensing authority to regulate such entities.

142. The LRA has reported that during the course of a tax audit they have never encountered foundations involved in tax evasion, tax avoidance or tax fraud schemes.

Conclusion

143. While there is no legal framework for foundations, the features of the "foundations" that may be established in Lesotho are not relevant for the work of the Global Forum.

Other relevant entities and arrangements

144. Under the Societies Act 20 of 1966, entities including clubs, companies, partnerships or associations of ten or more persons whatever its nature or object, can be registered as long as it is legal (s. 2), and does not conduct any business for " the acquisition of financial gain and of sharing the profit or loss between such persons" (s. 3). Notwithstanding, entities that can be registered under the Societies Act do not include those regulated by other legislation such as the Companies Act, Partnerships Proclamation or Friendly Societies Act. As of April 2016, there are 1 899 entities registered.

145. All entities registered under the Societies Act, are obligated to keep updated identity information on all members of the society as the information must be produced when requested at any time by the Registrar (s. 14(1)). Lesotho authorities have confirmed that such identity information of the members must be included in the rules of the society which may be in the form of a deed, instrument or document relating to the establishment, constitution, regulations, government, aims, objects, purposes and powers of a society (s. 2(3)). Information which may be requested by the Registrar includes the rules (or deed) of the society and a "true and complete list of office bearers and of the members of the society distinguishing those residing in Lesotho or present there" at the date of request (s. 14(1)(b)). Society returns, accounts and any other information may also be required (s. 14(1)(d)).The

persons obligated to maintain and supply the information are the president or chairman and secretary and every member of the committee or other governing body of a society (s. 15(1)). These provisions are enforced by penalties for failure to supply any of the information within the timeframe stipulated in the request (s. 15(2)). Such penalties include a fine up to LSL 200 (EUR12) or imprisonment up to six months (s. 28) and have never been applied in practice.

146. All records and registers relating to societies are to be kept at the Societies' Registry at Lesotho's capital of Maseru under the provisions of the Act (s. 5). All societies must be registered (s. 6) according to rules that may be prescribed by the Minister regarding the manner of registration, changes of name or objects, forms to be used, fees and annual returns and secures submission of accounts (s. 30).There is no provision in the Societies Act that deals with retention of information. However, Lesotho authorities have confirmed that the office of the Registrar General in practice keeps all information for 50 years in line with the governmental policy on retention of public records.

Conclusion

147. Lesotho's legal and regulatory framework ensures the availability of information on societies' members. While not expressly provided in the Societies Act, it may be reasonably expected and also confirmed by Lesotho authorities, that the obligations in the Act imply that societies must keep all required information, including identity information that may be requested by the Registrar. Societies are likely to be of more limited relevance for EOI as they generally don't conduct business. However, the fact that companies and partnerships can register under the Societies Act is enough to require Lesotho to have ownership and identity information of such entities. Lesotho authorities do not have regular oversight to monitor the compliance of obligations under the Societies Act and it is therefore recommended that Lesotho monitors the compliance of the legal obligations to maintain ownership and identity information of entities registered under the Societies Act and exercises its enforcement powers as appropriate to ensure that such information is available in practice.

Enforcement provisions to ensure availability of information (ToR A.1.6)

148. Lesotho should have in place effective enforcement provisions to ensure the availability of ownership and identity information. The existence of appropriate penalties for non-compliance with key obligations is an important tool for jurisdictions to effectively enforce the obligations to retain identity and ownership information.

149. The key enforcement provisions that apply on obligations to ensure the availability of ownership information are:

- Removal of a company by the Registrar from the register if the company fails to commence business within 12 months of incorporation, fails to submit an annual report, ceased its activities for 12 consecutive months, or if it has been absent at its registered address for 6 consecutive months (s. 87(5), Companies Act).This struck-off procedure was not used during the review period, but as of January 2016 there were 17 591 (17 029 private companies, 504 public companies and 58 foreign (external) companies) out of 29 030 companies altogether, have been struck-off from the Registry of Companies, *see A.1.1. Companies.*
- A company which fails to comply with the obligation to file notice of transfer of shares is liable to payment of a late filing fee of LSL 5 (EUR 0.29) for each day of failure to file such form (Schedule 7, Companies Regulations).There was no oversight conducted by the Registrar of Companies in this regard during the review period. Consequently, this penalty was never applied.
- Any person that fails to provide any records as requested by the Registrar is liable to conviction to a fine of LSL 20 000 (EUR 1 142) or imprisonment for 3 years, or both (s. 87(12), Companies Act). There was no oversight conducted by the Registrar of Companies in this regard during the review period. Consequently, this fine was never applied.
- An accountable institution which, or a person who, fails to comply with any AML requirements commits and offence, and is liable on conviction to, in the case of a natural person, imprisonment for a period not exceeding 10 years, or a fine of not less than LSL 50 000 (EUR 2 855) or both, and in the case of a legal person, a fine of not less than LSL 250 000 (EUR 14 274) (s. 26(3), MLPC Act). In addition or in the alternative to the fine mentioned above, the Court may order suspension or revocation of a business license (s. 26(4), MLPC Act).There was no oversight conducted by the FIU in respect of AML obligations during the review period. Consequently, these fines have never been applied or business licenses suspended or revoked.
- A person who fails to comply with the provisions of the Act commits an offence and where penalties are not provided for, such person shall be liable on conviction to a fine of not less that LSL 10 000 (EUR 571) or to imprisonment for a period not less than 30 months, and, in the case of a juristic person, a fine not less than LSL100 000(EUR 5708) (s. 113, MLPC Act).There was no oversight conducted by the FIU in

respect of AML obligations during the review period. Consequently, these fines were not applied during the review period.

- Any person who fails to file a return or document as required under the Income Tax Act, is guilty of an offence and liable on conviction to a fine not exceeding LSL 5 000 (EUR 370) or to imprisonment for a term not exceeding six months, or both (s. 175(1), Income Tax Act). This applies to all companies, trusts and partnerships. Lesotho was unable to provide statistics for sanctions imposed on companies, trusts and partnerships for failure to file annual tax returns during the review period.
- Any partnership that does not register or submit updated information on its partners will have no legal status and cannot enforce any rights arising out of any contract made or entered on behalf of any unregistered partnership (s. 28, Partnership Proclamation). Lesotho authorities have reported that they have never encountered in practice unregistered partnerships conducting business in Lesotho.
- Failure by any person to supply any of the information within the timeframe stipulated in the request by the Registrar-General under the Societies Act will result in an offence (s. 15) and liable to a fine up to LSL 200 (EUR 12) or imprisonment up to six months (s. 28). There was no oversight conducted by the Registrar-General in this regard during the review period. Consequently, this fine was never applied during the review period.

Conclusion

150. Enforcement provisions appear to be sufficient for domestic companies, foreign (external) companies, partnerships and societies. For trusts, there is no specific law that governs trusts but common law fiduciary duties may be sufficient and enforcement provisions under tax and AML laws are sufficient to the extent where the trusts have taxable income or where AML-covered financial institutions or company service providers are involved in the administration of the trusts.

151. Domestic and foreign (external) companies were not regularly monitored during the review period. However in December 2015 a programme was put in place to monitor compliance of the obligations in the Companies Act. As a result, there were 17 591 (17 029 private companies, 504 public companies and 58 foreign (external) companies) out of 29 030 companies altogether, were struck off from the Companies Registry and new regular oversight programme was established to systematically monitor compliance with these obligations. Lesotho should monitor the implementation of this new oversight programme and exercise its enforcement powers as appropriate

to ensure that ownership and identity information for domestic and external companies is available in practice.

152. Enforcement measures have never been applied in practice to ensure that partnerships and trusts comply with their obligations to keep ownership and identity information. Lesotho should put in place an oversight programme to ensure compliance with the obligations to maintain ownership and identity information of partnerships, any type of trusts and societies, and exercise its enforcement powers as appropriate to ensure that such information is available in practice. The element has been determined as in place but certain aspects of the legal implementation needing improvement and rated as "Partially Compliant".

Determination and factors underlying recommendations

Phase 1 determination	
The element is in place, but certain aspects of the legal implementation of the element need improvement.	
Factors underlying recommendations	**Recommendations**
While there are no share warrants to bearer in circulation at present, the mechanisms in place may be insufficient to ensure the availability of identity information of all holders of share warrants.	Lesotho should take steps to ensure that robust mechanisms are in place to identify owners of share warrants to bearer or eliminate companies' ability to issue such share warrants.

Phase 2 Rating	
Partially Compliant	
Factor underlying recommendation	**Recommendations**
Domestic and external companies were not regularly monitored during the review period. However in December 2015 a programme was put in place to monitor compliance of the obligations in the Companies Act. As a result, 17 591 out of 29 030 companies were struck off from the Companies Registry and a new regular oversight programme was established to systematically monitor compliance with these obligations.	Lesotho should monitor the implementation of this new oversight programme and exercise its enforcement powers as appropriate to ensure that ownership and identity information for domestic and foreign (external) companies is available in practice.

Phase 2 Rating	
Partially Compliant	
Factor underlying recommendation	**Recommendations**
Lesotho authorities do not have regular oversight to monitor the compliance of legal obligations to ensure that ownership and identity information is available for general partnerships, any types of trusts (including voting trusts) and societies. Existing enforcement provisions to ensure that ownerships and identity information is available for these type of entities or arrangements have never been applied in practice.	Lesotho should put in place an oversight programme to ensure compliance with the obligations to maintain ownership and identity information of partnerships, all types of trusts and societies, and exercise its enforcement powers as appropriate to ensure that such information is available in practice.

A.2. Accounting records

> Jurisdictions should ensure that reliable accounting records are kept for all relevant entities and arrangements.

153. The Terms of Reference sets out the standards for the maintenance of reliable accounting records and the necessary accounting record retention period. They provide that reliable accounting records should be kept for all relevant entities and arrangements. To be reliable, accounting records should: *(i)* correctly explain all transactions; *(ii)* enable the financial position of the entity or arrangement to be determined with reasonable accuracy at any time; and *(iii)* allow financial statements to be prepared. Accounting records should further include underlying documentation, such as invoices, contracts, etc. Accounting records need to be kept for a minimum of five years.

General requirements (ToR A.2.1), Underlying documentation (ToR A.2.2) and 5-year retention standard (ToR A.2.3)

Companies

154. The Companies Act and Income Tax Act both provide obligations for companies to keep accounting records.

155. Under the Companies Act, accounting records is listed as a mandatory item of the company records that all companies must maintain at its registered office or at some other place in Lesotho (s. 84(1)). All accounting records are to be kept in English or Sesotho, in written form or a form easily

accessible and convertible into written form, and in Lesotho (s. 84(3), 96(3)). These requirements apply to all companies, domestic companies, and to external companies that carry on a business in Lesotho and are thus registered with the Registrar (s. 2(1)).

156. The requirements in Lesotho regarding accounting records are in line with the standard under A.2.1. Under the Companies Act, the board of the company must keep accounting records that *(a)* correctly reflect and explain the financial transactions of the company; *(b)* provide the financial position of the company at any time with reasonable accuracy; and *(c)* enable the accounts of the company to be readily available for audit purposes (s. 96(1)). "Accounts" is interpreted as annual financial statements (s. 2(1)).

157. The financial statements must be audited by a qualified auditor in accordance to the Companies Act (s. 97). This obligation is imposed on all companies except for some private companies which have less than 10 shareholders, is a single shareholding company, where none of the shareholders is a company or if majority of shareholders agree not to appoint an auditor (s. 98(3)). Notwithstanding, private companies are still subjected to the obligations applicable to all companies to keep detailed accounting records which must be readily available for inspection by any director or shareholder of the company. For all companies, the board of the company must prepare and file an annual report with the Registrar annually within three months of the anniversary date of its incorporation (s. 105(3)). Amongst other items, the annual report must contain all financial statements, the auditor's report, where applicable, and describe any change in accounting policies (s. 105(1)). Companies are also required under the Income Tax Act to submit the financial statements together with their tax returns which are to be filed by their nominated officers (s. 128 and Income Tax Return form).

158. The detailed accounting records that must be kept by companies as provided under the Companies Act, complemented with the Income Tax Act, are in line with the standard under A.2.2 regarding underlying documentation. The accounting records of all companies must contain *(a)* entries of money received and money spent each day and the matters to which it relates; *(b)* a record of the assets and liabilities of the company; *(c)* if the company's business involves dealing in goods, a record of physical stock held at the end of the financial year together with stock records if any during the year; and *(d)* if the company's business involves providing services, a record of services provided and relevant invoices and documents (s. 96(2)). The Income Tax Act also requires that all taxpayers maintain in Lesotho any records necessary for the accurate determination of the tax payable by the taxpayer (s. 169(1)).

159. Regarding the retention requirement for accounting records, Lesotho is in line with the standard under A.2.3. Companies are to keep accounting records required under the Companies Act for the last 10 completed financial

years of the company, and copies of all accounts (annual financial statements) for the last 10 completed financial years of the company (s. 84(1)(i) and (j)).

160. The following enforcement provisions in the Companies Act and Income Tax Act help ensure the availability of accounting records:

Companies Act:

- The board of the company must ensure that financial statements are prepared annually and audited, or may otherwise be sued by its shareholders (s. 94).
- Where a company fails to submit its regular annual report along with the financial statements (s. 108), the company may be removed from the register of companies (s. 87(5)), and/or subject to a penalty as may be determined by the Minister (S. 185(2)).

Income Tax Act:

- Failure to file a return or document required, and/or to maintain proper records in accordance with the requirements of the Income Tax Act is an offence and the nominated officer of the company would be liable on conviction to a fine not exceeding LSL 10 000 (EUR 575) or to imprisonment for a term not exceeding two years, or both (S. 176).

161. In addition to the Companies Act, the Income Tax Act also contains accounting information obligations for all taxpayers, including companies, partnerships, trusts and foundations. As the provisions pertaining to accounting information under the Companies Act appear to be adequate for purposes of the standard, the provisions under the Income Tax Act will also be further analysed in the subsequent sections as regards to ensuring the availability of accounting information for partnerships, trusts and foundations.

Partnerships

162. The obligations under the Income Tax Act regarding the keeping of accounting information apply to all taxpayers including companies, partnerships and trusts. Some obligations for partnerships to keep accounting information are also provided under the Partnerships Proclamation of 1957.

163. Under the Partnerships Proclamation, there are some general requirements for partnerships to keep accounting information. Partnerships are required to have information on each partner's duties and degree of participation in the partnership business, and sufficient information to draw up balance sheets within six months after the formation of the partnership and

thereafter at annual intervals, accounts of the profits and losses, custody of partnership funds and the accounting and auditing of partnership books (s. 5(1)(i) to (o)). The balance sheets required are interpreted by Lesotho authorities as the financial statements. All partnerships, including non-resident (foreign) partnerships, carrying on a business in Lesotho are required under the Income Tax Act to submit the financial statements together with their tax returns which are to be filed by their nominated officers (s. 128 and Income Tax Return form).

164. The obligation to keep records is placed with the nominated officer of the partnership who is required to be resident where there are issues of non-residence by one or other partners (s. 211(1) and (2), Income Tax Act). This implies that all accounting information on partnerships is to be kept in Lesotho.

165. The Income Tax Act also provides that records or evidence which are necessary for the accurate determination of tax payable by the taxpayer must be retained by the taxpayer for so long as they remain material in the administration of the Act (s. 169). Guidance on the underlying documentation that has to be kept by partnerships and trusts is provided in the Explanatory Memorandum to the Income Tax Act. The "records" that has to be retained by all taxpayers is intended to be interpreted broadly covering all written documents which record and explain the transactions and other acts of the taxpayer that are relevant to the determination of the taxpayer's liability. This not only includes records relevant to the ascertainment of the taxpayer's chargeable income and tax credits, but also records relating to any election, estimate, determination, or calculation made by the taxpayer for the purposes of the Income Tax Act. The records must be kept in a manner, which is sufficiently detailed and logically consistent so as to enable a person of reasonable competence to ascertain the taxpayer's liability promptly, easily and quickly (s. 169 of the Explanatory Memorandum).These requirements appear sufficient in meeting the standard under A.2.2 as Lesotho authorities have confirmed that the records would include detailed contacts and invoices that reflect all sums of money received and expended, all sales and purchases by the partnership and the assets and liability of the partnership.

166. The Partnership Proclamation does not have specific provisions on the length of time in which documents should be maintained. Nevertheless, under the Income Tax Act, information must be retained by taxpayer "for so long as they remain material in the administrations of the Act" (s. 169), which would entail keeping information for a minimum of five years since the time limit for which any tax assessments can be made or amended is four years after the notice is served at the end of the year of assessment (s. 135).

167. Similar to companies, there are enforcement provisions under the Income Tax Act where failure to file a return or document required, and/or to

maintain proper records in accordance with the requirements of the Income Tax Act is an offence and the nominated officer of the company would be liable on conviction to a fine not exceeding LSL 10 000 (EUR 571) or to imprisonment for a term not exceeding two years, or both (S. 176). There are no enforcement provisions for the obligations under the Partnerships Proclamation.

Trusts

168. The accounting record keeping obligations on companies and partnerships under the Income Tax Act similarly apply to trusts that carry on a business in Lesotho or have taxable income. In addressing the three elements under the standard (A.2.1, A.2.2 and A.2.3), this includes the requirements to prepare and submit financial statements along with the annual tax returns (s. 128), the type of "records" that must be maintained (s. 169) and for information to be retained "for so long as they remain material in the administrations of the Act" (s. 169)which would entail keeping information for a minimum of five years since the time limit for which any tax assessments can be made or amended is four years after the notice is served at the end of the year of assessment (s. 135). The enforcement provisions for companies and partnerships under the Income Tax Act also apply to trusts (s. 176). Under the Income Tax Act, all trusts that carry on a business in Lesotho or have taxable income are required to file a trust return of income (s. 81(7)) regardless whether income or loss has been made.

169. However, as analysed in A.1, there appears to be a gap in relying on the Income Tax Act to ensure the availability of accounting information. For trusts that do not ever receive taxable income, these trusts would not have been required to file a tax return and would not be subjected to the accounting record keeping obligations in the Income Tax Act. This would refer to trusts which receive only foreign-source income and has a non-resident settlor. Lesotho authorities have clarified that since Lesotho taxes on the worldwide income for its residents, the onus would be on the resident trustee to keep all relevant accounting information to prove that all the trust income does not accrue to him/her to avoid being taxed. However, there are no express provisions that ensure that all trusts that exist in Lesotho would have to be registered with the tax authorities regardless of its taxable status, and therefore subjected to all obligations of the Income Tax Act. As such, it is not clear if accounting record keeping obligations would be observed by trustees of trusts that do not ever receive taxable income. Lesotho should ensure that all trusts in Lesotho maintain accounting records even where the trust is not carrying on business or is not subject to tax in Lesotho.

170. While there is no specific law for trusts, the obligation for the trustee to keep accounting records arises from common law requirements. Under common law, all trustees resident in Lesotho are subject to a broad fiduciary

duty to the beneficiaries to keep proper records and accounts of their trusteeship. Lesotho authorities also advised that with regard to the accounting records that must be prepared or maintained as part of the trustees' fiduciary duty, the accounting standards under the International Financial Reporting Standards that are applicable in Lesotho will apply. These standards are also espoused in the accounting record keeping obligations which companies are subjected to under the Companies Act, and which as assessed, meets the international standard in terms of the accounting information and underlying documentation to be kept, and the minimum retention period.

Societies

171. The Societies Act provides requirements for societies to keep "accounts relating to the assets and liabilities and income and expenditure" (s. 30(1)(d)). In addition, it may be reasonable to infer that societies must also keep this accounting information available at all times to be submitted whenever requested by the Registrar General for "such accounts, returns and other information as he may think fit" (s. 14(d), Societies Act). Societies is also covered under the Income Tax Act definition of "companies" (s. 3(1))[5] and would be subjected to all record-keeping obligations under the Income Tax Act, which as analysed in the preceding sections, meet the requirements of the international standard.

Availability of accounting records in practice

172. The Companies Act prescribes obligations for all domestic and foreign (external) companies to maintain reliable accounting records. The extent to which entities comply with the accounting requirements under the Companies Act is unknown in practice as officials from the Registrar of Companies have reported that during the review period, there was no system of oversight in place to monitor the companies' obligations to maintain accounting information under the Companies Act. However, recently a systematic oversight programme was put in place to ensure that companies comply with all obligations prescribed by the Companies Act, including the annual filing of financial statements. Lesotho should monitor the implementation of this new oversight programme and exercise its enforcement powers as appropriate to ensure that accounting information for domestic and foreign (external) companies is available in practice.

173. Nevertheless, companies and all other relevant entities, including partnerships and trusts – except those with a non-resident settlor and which

5. "Company" means a body corporate or unincorporate, whether created or recognised under the law in force in Lesotho or elsewhere (s. 3(1), Income Tax Act).

do not receive taxable income in Lesotho –, are subject to the accounting record requirements of the Income Tax Act These entities are required to submit financial statements together with the tax return each year (s. 128) and failure to do so will result in a fine not exceeding LSL 10 000 or for imprisonment for a term not exceeding two years, or both (s. 176).

174. Compliance levels for companies and partnerships filing annual tax returns were as follows. These figures are provided as at December 2015 and as such includes information from all companies that were struck-off in January 2016, see A.1.1 *Companies*. Companies that failed to file annual tax returns in the previous years were among those that have now been struck off from the Companies Registry. It is therefore expected that tax filing compliance levels will increase in 2016 and thereafter. Tax filing compliance of annual tax returns for partnerships is low in Lesotho, but there are currently only 236 partnerships.

	2013	2014	2015
Private companies	55%	60%	60%
Public companies	60%	65%	66%
Partnerships	19%	25%	26%

175. With regard to trusts, Lesotho was unable to provide compliance rates for trusts filing annual tax returns because trusts can be registered under any business sector and as such, are placed in different categories. Lesotho has reported that trusts are usually placed within the private companies category and so compliance levels are generally those of private companies.

176. The availability of accounting records, including underlying documentation, is furthered monitored by the LRA under its regular surveillance programme in place. The LRA has reported that in the course of their inspections, amongst the documents they examine are the financial statements and accounting records maintained by the entity. The LRA also verifies in the course of these inspections, that the minimum retention periods for accounting records, including underlying documentation, are complied with.

177. The following types of audits conducted by the LRA may require checking financial statements and accounting records: refund audits, verification audits, limited scope audits and intensive audits. Refund audits are performed to ensure that any refunds to be refunded by LRA are valid and accurate. The refund audit comprises the verification of those areas on a value added tax and income tax return that gave rise to the refund and is carried out as desk audits by means of correspondence with taxpayers. Accounting records and financial statements might be requested from the

taxpayer to verify the information provided by the taxpayer before any refund is granted by the LRA.

178. Verification audits are short visits by an auditor to the taxpayer to verify a particular aspect of the tax return. The verification in this regard may be focused on one tax type only. These visits can last up to a working day and in order to verify the particular aspect under surveillance the auditors can request the taxpayer to provide copy of their accounting records that support the tax return being verified.

179. In limited scope audits surveillance is confined to specific issues in respect of a tax return filed or a specific area of the law. The objective is to examine key risk areas of non-compliance. Books and records will always be examined in these cases and, because of time constraints, Auditors will focus on areas of risk only, having initially verified the turnover figures. Limited scope audit may give rise to a Comprehensive audit if the Auditor uncovers information that leads him to believe that a more detailed examination of records is required. In cases of fraud or large scale evasion, Auditors should not leave the records in the hands of the taxpayer as there is a strong possibility of these being amended. In exceptional cases the Auditor should remove all books and records for further examination in the office. Limited scope audits should never exceed five full days in duration.

180. Comprehensive audits include examination of all or most information relevant to the calculation of the taxpayer's liability for a given period. It covers every aspect of the business. The majority of risk areas are examined and the objective is to determine the correct tax liability for the return as a whole. These should always be preceded by a well thought out audit plan which will highlight the particular areas of risk that should be examined. Comprehensive audits may last five to twenty one days. During the course of comprehensive audits accounting information is always verified.

181. Over the review period, the number of audits performed by LRA is as follows:

Year	Number of onsite inspections
2012 (Jul-Dec)	22
2013	35
2014	14
2015	84

182. In the course of performing onsite inspections, auditors have reported to have found a high level of compliance with accounting record requirements. In the case where breaches with obligations under the Income Tax Act

were found, the LRA proceeded to impose the corresponding fines. The total amount of fines imposed by the LRA over the review period is as follows:

Year	Total amount of fines imposed (LSL)*
2012 (Jun-Dec)	23 250 810
2013	52 330 084
2014	969 268
2015	18 030 435

* The totals for the fines imposed over the review period are aggregate numbers and not all fines relate directly to non-compliance with requirements to maintain accounting information.

183. Lesotho has reported that during 2014 most of the LRA efforts were concentrated in a tax modernisation project and this is why audits in 2014 decreased. The tax modernisation project's objectives are to enhance tax revenue collection, enable a single view of the taxpayer along with the other systems of the Integrated Revenue Management System, streamline service to taxpayers through and improve efficiency of the LRA tax collection processes. The project was launched in 2015 and Lesotho informed that results are already showing. Lesotho should monitor the implementation of this project and exercise their auditing and enforcement powers as appropriate to ensure that accounting information is available in practice.

184. In respect to trusts that only receive foreign-source income and where the settlor is a non-resident, the LRA has reported that in practice they have never encountered one in the course of a tax audit. Further, over the review period, Lesotho did not receive any request for accounting information of trusts.

Conclusion

185. The legal framework in Lesotho concerning the accounting record keeping obligations and the enforcement provisions appear to be sufficient to meet the standard to a large extent. Companies are subjected to rules sufficiently laid out in the Companies Act, which is also supported by similar obligations under the Income Tax Act. Partnerships, trusts and foundations are subjected to all record-keeping obligations under the Income Tax Act, including the requirement to keep underlying documentation and for information to be retained for a minimum of five years. As analysed above, these obligations meet the requirements of the international standard. However, a gap exists as regards to trusts that do not receive taxable income in Lesotho,

and thus not subjected to the obligations under the Income Tax Act and common law fiduciary duty by itself may not be sufficient to ensure the availability of accounting information.

186. The LRA monitors compliance with the accounting recordkeeping obligations prescribed by the tax laws but this supervision is limited to registered taxpayers, which include domestic and foreign (external) companies, partnerships and trusts deriving income in Lesotho. The availability of accounting records in practice is monitored through the filing of annual tax returns and through the LRA's regular oversight programme which covers that the accounting requirements, including underlying documentation, prescribed by the Income Tax Act are complied with. However, trusts that only receive foreign-source income and where the settlor is a non-resident are not covered by the oversight that LRA conducts. It is, therefore, recommended that Lesotho puts in place a comprehensive oversight programme to ensure compliance with and enforcement of the obligation to maintain reliable accounting records and underlying documents for all relevant entities and arrangements.

187. Over the review period, Lesotho received one request regarding accounting information pertaining to a company. Lesotho was able to retrieve this information from its databases. Feedback from peers indicates that they were satisfied with the accounting information provided by Lesotho during the review period. Element A.2 has determined to be in place, but certain aspects of the legal implementation needing improvement and rated as "Largely compliant".

Determination and factors underlying recommendations

Phase 1 determination	
The element is in place, but certain aspects of the legal implementation of the element need improvement.	
Factors underlying recommendations	**Recommendations**
Only trusts that receive taxable income would be subjected to obligations under the Income Tax Act to keep accounting records. The availability of accounting information is not ensured for trusts that receive only foreign-source income and where the settlor is non-resident.	Lesotho should ensure the availability of accounting records of all trusts in Lesotho even where the trust is not carrying on business or is not subject to tax in Lesotho.

Phase 2 Rating	
Largely Compliant	
Factors underlying recommendations	**Recommendations**
Lesotho authorities monitor compliance with the accounting record keeping obligations prescribed by the tax laws but this supervision is limited to registered taxpayers, which include domestic and foreign (external) companies, partnerships and trusts deriving income in Lesotho. There is a regular oversight programme which covers that the accounting requirements prescribed by the Income Tax Act are complied with. However, the compliance level for partnerships is low and trusts that only receive foreign-source income and where the settlor is a non-resident are not covered by the oversight that LRA conducts.	Lesotho should put in place a comprehensive oversight programme to ensure compliance with and enforcement of the obligation to maintain reliable accounting records and underlying documents for all relevant entities and arrangements.

A.3. Banking Information

Banking information should be available for all account-holders.

188. Access to banking information is of interest to the tax administration when the bank has useful and reliable information about its customers' identity and the nature and amount of their financial transactions.

Record-keeping requirements (ToRA.3.1)

189. Lesotho has a small financial sector dominated by subsidiaries of South African financial institutions. There are four commercial banks in Lesotho. The CBL is the regulatory and supervisory authority of all banks and administers the relevant laws for the establishment of banks and record-keeping obligations – Financial Institutions Act of 2012 ("FI Act") and the Central Bank Act of 2000.

190. Banking businesses in Lesotho or abroad by a local financial institution require a licence issued by the Commissioner under the FI Act (s. 5(1)). Financial institutions refer to deposit-taking (banks) and non-deposit taking

institutions (s. 2). Failure to obtain a license and the carrying out of unauthorised business is an offence and the person (director or an officer of the body corporate) may be liable to a fine of LSL 20 000 (EUR 1 143) and/or imprisonment for one year (s. 5). To obtain a license, banks must also be incorporated as a public company under the Companies Act, are thereby also subjected to all registration and record-keeping requirements under the Companies Act (s. 5(2), FI Act).

191. Accepting deposits from the public is only allowed in Lesotho if the person is licensed to do so under the FI Act (s. 11(4)). Any person who contravenes this provision commits an offence and shall, on conviction, be liable to a fine of LSL 40000 (EUR 2 284) or to imprisonment for a term of two years. In the case of a body corporation, the term of imprisonment shall apply to any director, officer or person responsible for carrying out such unauthorised act (s. 11(6)).

192. Under the FI Act, banks are obligated to prepare financial statements in accordance to the internationally accepted accounting standards adopted by the accounting bodies in Lesotho (s. 39). Record-keeping obligations by banks include:

- Accounting records exhibiting clearly and correctly the state of its business affairs, explaining its transactions and financial position so as to enable the commissioner to determine whether the financial institution has complied with all provisions of the FI Act (s. 40(2)(a)),
- Financial statements (s. 40(2)(b)),
- Records showing, for each customer, at least on a daily basis, particulars of its transactions with or for the account of that customer, and the balance owing to or by that customer (s. 40(2)(c)).
- Keeping of records for a period at least 10 years after the completion of the transaction to which relates (s. 40(3)(b)),
- Records are to be at the principal office or other location of the financial institution in Lesotho (s. 40(2)(d)),
- Records which are kept by a third party must be easily accessible and available within three days ((s. 40(4)).
- Submit audited financial statements, balance sheet and profit and loss statements within three months after the end of a financial year (s. 41). All financial statements to be signed by principal officers, directors, manager and next senior manager for local institutions and foreign institutions, whichever applies, to the Commissioner.

193. All banks are also "accountable institutions" of the MLPC Act and must adhere to the AML and KYC regulations in the MLPC Act and accompanying Money Laundering Notices. Financial Institutions as defined in the Financial Institution Act 1999 (replaced by the Financial Institutions Act of 2012) must adhere to the Anti-Money Laundering requirements as specified in Part III of the Act (s. 2 (1) and part III).

194. Under the MLPC Act, banks, when establishing a business relationship, obtain information on the purpose and nature of the business relationship and, if the transaction is conducted by a natural person, adequately identify and verify his or her identity including information relating to the individual's name, address and occupation and the national identity card or passport or other applicable official identifying document (s. 16(1)). In the case of a transaction conducted by a legal entity, banks should adequately identify and verify its legal existence and structure, including information relating to the customer's name, legal status, address and directors and the principal owners and beneficiaries and control structure of the entity. In addition the banks should establish the provisions regulating the power to bind the entity and verify that any person purporting to act on behalf of the customer is so authorised, and identify those persons (s. 16(1)).

195. The KYC procedures applicable to banks are further described in the Money Laundering (Accountable Institutions) Guidelines, Legal Notice no. 55 of 2013 (the AML Guidelines). In accordance to the guidelines, banks should obtain and verify particulars of identity of trustees, nominees, or fiduciaries and the underlying beneficiary on whose behalf a business transaction is entered into, and establish the purpose of which the transaction is entered into (s. 6(4)(b)). In addition, banks are obliged to obtain and verify the identity of a third party if the deposit is by, or on behalf of, a third party (s. 13).

196. The Guidelines further specify that in the case where a business relationship is conducted through an account, banks shall obtain and verify the particulars of the identity of the customer or client at the time the banking of deposit account is opened. In cases where the business relationship is conducted on a one-off basis, the bank shall obtain and verify the particulars of the identity of the customer or client at the time the transaction occurs, unless the deposit to, or by, the customer or client is less than LSL 20 000 (EUR1 143).

197. The AML Guidelines state that where verification of the customer's or client's identity is satisfactorily completed, further verification shall not be necessary when the customer or client subsequently undertakes transactions as long as regular contact with the customer or client is maintained (s12(1)). Nonetheless, the AML Guidelines specify that banks shall monitor its customers or clients and their transactions on an on-going basis and observe the

collection and verification of additional KYC information in relation to on-going customer due diligence (s. 16(1)).

198. Where evidence of a person's identity is obtained in accordance with section 16 of the MLPC Act, a record that indicates the nature of the evidence obtained, and which comprises either a copy of the evidence or such information as would enable a copy of it to be obtained shall be maintained by the banks (s. 17(1)). The obligation to maintain records is further described in the AML Guidelines where it is stated that banks shall keep and maintain records of its customers or clients' business transactions that contain daily records of transactions, receipts, paying-in books, customer or client correspondence and cheques. Such records shall be kept for a minimum of 5 years from when the business transaction is conducted (s. 17(1)). In addition the AML Guidelines stipulate that an accountable institution shall ensure that documents used to verify the identity of the customer or client and documents or information used to verify the identity of the beneficial owners are kept (s. 17(3)(c)). The records should also include records of on-going monitoring, documents or information on correspondent banking relationships and documentation on reliance on third parties among other things (s. 17(3)). Such records should be kept by the accountable institution for a period of at least 5 years from the date the relevant business or transaction was completed, or termination of business relationship, whichever is the later (MLPC Act s. 17(4)).

199. Banks which fail to comply with any AML requirements commits an offence, and shall be liable on conviction to, in the case of a natural person, imprisonment for a period not exceeding 10 years, or a fine of not less than LSL 50 000 (EUR 2 856) or both, and in the case of a legal person, a fine of not less than LSL 250 000 (EUR 14 285) (s. 26(3)). In addition or in the alternative to the fine mentioned above the Court may order suspension or revocation of a business license (s. 26(4)).

Availability of banking information in practice

200. The legal obligations in place to maintain banking information, under both the FI Act and the MLPC Act require banks to maintain account holder and transaction information. The CBL is the body responsible for the licensing and the on-going supervision of all banks and deposit-taking institutions. As of April 2016, there were four commercial banks under the supervision of the CBL. Supervision is conducted by the Supervision Division, which comprises 51 officials responsible for the ongoing oversight programme.

201. All commercial Banks in Lesotho are subject to comprehensive examination at least once per year. Examination entails an on-site inspection which usually takes six weeks. All branches are also visited during the

on-site inspection. Supervision in general is conducted using the supervisory rating system known as "Uniform Financial Institutions Rating System" in which the following six components are assessed: capital adequacy, asset quality, management capabilities, earnings quality and level, liquidity adequacy and sensitivity to market risk. The CBL informed that while minor breaches (i.e. those that do not threaten the stability of the bank of the banking system) have been found, generally compliance with regulatory and legal requirements is very high.

202. In regards to obligations under the MLPC Act, specifically those relating to KYC, the CBL has reported that these are not examined in detail in the course of their inspections since supervision of KYC should be conducted by the FIU. The FIU conveyed that their compliance department is very new and since its creation, they have been working towards addressing the recommendations on their 2010 Mutual Evaluation on Anti-Money Laundering and Combating the Financing of Terrorism conducted by the ESAAMLG. The FIU started conducting compliance activities in 2015 through the supervision of suspicious transactions and reported to have visited a bank to audit AML obligations in November 2015. Accordingly, during the review period, the FIU did not conduct any supervision of accountable institutions.

Conclusion

203. The legal and regulatory framework in Lesotho requires the availability of banking information to the standard. Identity information on all account-holders is made available through specific provision in the FI Act and AML obligations and the availability of transaction records is primarily ensured by the FI Act as well as accounting and AML rules. Commercial banks are closely monitored by CBL. However, CBL does not supervise in detail AML obligations as supervision of these obligations is conducted by the FIU. The FIU has reported that their compliance division is very new and that no oversight was carried out during the review period. Consequently, no enforcement measures were applied for non-compliance of AML obligations by banks regarding their customer due diligence requirements.

204. Over the review period, Lesotho received one request for banking information. Lesotho provided this information to its EOI partner after obtaining it from a bank. Considering the above, element A.3 is determined to be "in place" and rated as "Largely Compliant".

Determination and factors underlying recommendations

Phase 1 determination
The element is in place.

Phase 2 Rating	
Largely Compliant	
Factor underlying recommendation	**Recommendations**
During the review period there was no oversight on compliance of AML regulations by banks regarding their customer due diligence requirements.	Lesotho should put in place an oversight programme to ensure compliance with AML regulations and effectively apply enforcement measures on banks regarding their customer due diligence requirements.

B. Access to information

Overview

205. A variety of information may be needed in a tax enquiry and jurisdictions should have the authority to obtain all such information. This includes information held by banks and other financial institutions as well as information concerning the ownership of companies or the identity of interest holders in other persons or entities, such as partnerships and trusts, as well as accounting information in respect of all such entities. This section of the report examines whether Lesotho's legal and regulatory framework gives the authorities access powers that cover the right types of persons and information and whether rights and safeguards would be compatible with effective exchange of information.

206. The Lesotho competent authority has broad access powers to obtain and provide requested information held by persons within its territorial jurisdiction. All information gathering powers which can be used for domestic purposes can be used for EOI purposes regardless whether there is a domestic tax interest. Lesotho has in place enforcement provisions to compel the production of information, including criminal sanctions and search and seizure power. Professional privilege under common law only protects communication produced for purposes of seeking or providing legal advice or use in existing or contemplated legal proceedings.

207. Lesotho's law does not require the tax authorities to notify taxpayers or third parties of an exchange of information request, or when the tax authority collects information from a third party to fulfil an exchange of information request. There are also no specific legal provisions allowing the taxpayer to appeal the exchange of information.

208. Overall, the legal and regulatory framework in Lesotho is in line with the international standard to allow the competent authority to access all information for EOI purposes.

B.1. Competent Authority's ability to obtain and provide information

> Competent authorities should have the power to obtain and provide information that is the subject of a request under an exchange of information arrangement from any person within their territorial jurisdiction who is in possession or control of such information (irrespective of any legal obligation on such person to maintain the secrecy of the information).

209. The competent authority in Lesotho for EOI purposes is the Commissioner General of the LRA. The Commissioner General has general administration of the Income Tax Act (s. 200(2)). The Commissioner General is the competent authority to gather and provide the requested information for EOI purposes. The Commissioner General has wide powers to do that including gathering information directly from the taxpayer, third persons and other government authorities.

210. The ITD Section serves under the Legal and Policy Division which in turn serves under the Lesotho competent authority. The ITD Section is headed by a Manager and has one additional staff member. All EOI requests received by the competent authority are processed by the ITD Section which is in turn supervised by the Manager of the Legal and Policy Division.

Bank, ownership and identity information (ToR B.1.1) and Accounting records (ToR B.1.2)

211. The Commissioner General's (or any authorised officer's) information gathering powers include the following:

- full and free access to any premises, place, book, record, or computer and to make an extract or copy at all times and without prior notice (s. 170(1)(a) and (b), ITA);
- seize and retain such information as above for purposes of enforcement of the Income Tax Act (s. 170(c), ITA);
- be provided all assistance by any persons on the premises or place where the Commissioner General must exercise effective power to obtain or examine information (s. 170(3));
- issue a notice to require any person "whether a taxpayer or not", to produce any document or record described in the notice (s. 171(1));
- issue a notice to require any person "whether taxpayer or not" to be examined under oath and give evidence regarding the tax affairs of that person or of any other person, as well as produce any book, record, or computer-stored information in their control (s. 171(2)).

212. While it is not expressly stated in the Income Tax Act, Lesotho authorities interpret that its information gathering powers under these two

sections would be used by the Commissioner General to obtain information for EOI purposes. The powers under section 170 applies "in order to enforce the provisions of this Act", thus permitting the Commissioner General to obtain information from any person. However, this language may be limited to Lesotho's domestic tax purposes, given that the provision refers specifically to "this Act". Notwithstanding, section 171 provides for clearer and broader access by the Commissioner General to "by notice in writing, require any person, whether a taxpayer or not" to provide any information "as may be required by the notice" (s. 171(1), (2)). There is no restriction under section 171 that the powers are to be used with respect to enforcing the provisions of "this Act". The Explanatory Memorandum also confirms that this section "provides the Commissioner General with a general power to obtain information from any person", and thus does not appear to limit the application to only relevant persons, i.e. taxpayers, and for purposes of enforcing provisions of the Income Tax Act. While the law is silent on whether these powers under section 171 can be used for non-domestic tax purposes, the distinction made in section 170 "to enforce the provisions of this Act" infers that section 171 could thus be applied more broadly to cover all persons, regardless of any domestic tax purpose.

213. Lesotho authorities have also confirmed that these powers under section 171 are to be applied if information is to be sought for EOI purpose under the avoidance of double taxation agreements entered into by the Government of Lesotho in accordance to s. 112(1) of the Income Tax Act. "Avoidance of double taxation agreement" is defined to include "an agreement with a foreign government providing for reciprocal administrative assistance in the enforcement of tax liabilities" (s. 112(4), Income Tax Act) which Lesotho authorities have applied in practice as including agreements that provide for exchange of information, such as TIEAs and other multilateral agreements that may include provisions for EOI. It may be reasonable to read this as establishing a duty of the Commissioner General to use its information gathering powers to render such assistance for EOI under an applicable agreement, despite that the Income Tax Act is silent to this effect. Lesotho authorities also indicate that the Commissioner General's broader information gathering powers under section 171 can be applied for EOI purposes in view of the treaty prevail rule that is elaborated in the Explanatory Memorandum to section 112 of the Income Tax Act that "the terms of any treaty (such as a double tax treaty) or international agreement to which Lesotho is a party… prevail over the Order (Income Tax Act)".

214. The Commissioner General's information gathering powers under section 171 are therefore sufficiently broad and is accompanied by compulsory powers where any person who fails to comply with a notice is guilty of an offence and liable on conviction to a fine not exceeding LSL 5 000 (EUR 286) and/or imprisonment for a term of up to six months (s. 183, Income Tax Act).

215. Lesotho authorities have also confirmed that these powers under section 171can be used for EOI and are applicable for directly obtaining information from any persons who may have in their possession any information that the Commissioner General may require. This includes information on all relevant entities for EOI regardless if they are subjected to tax. There is no specific information gathering powers intended solely for EOI. There are also no specific procedures or additional conditions for use of information gathering powers in respect of different types of information. Lesotho authorities also indicate that all information is obtainable through the issuance of the notice by the Commissioner General. There are no other special procedures required under the law, such as application for a court order or warrant for obtaining information from any specific persons.

216. Additionally, the FIU is mandated to obtain information on all suspicious activities, including ownership and identity information. If tax matters are identified on the basis of its analysis, then the FIU will pass on such information to LRA. This is its mandate under anti-money laundering measures, which prescribe that the authority may transmit any information obtained where there was suspicion of commission of an offence and derived from such examination to the appropriate domestic or foreign law enforcement authority or supervisory authorities if there are reasonable grounds to suspect relevance to an investigation (s. 12, MLPC Act).

Information gathering measures in practice

217. There are no different processes involved where an EOI request is received pursuant to a double tax convention, tax information exchange agreement or administrative assistance agreement. Over the three-year review period, the LRA experienced no undue delays or practical difficulties when exercising access powers to gather information from other agencies, the taxpayer or third parties. The procedures are generally the same irrespective of the kind of information requested, or whether it relates to criminal or administrative investigation.

218. All EOI requests are received and processed by ITD, who before having in place the Exchange of Information Standard Operating Procedure (EOI Manual), would forward the request on to the Investigation Unit that serves under the Enforcement Division. Investigation would assist gathering the requested information. If the information is readily available in one of the institutional databases of the LRA, the Investigations Unit will prepare a memorandum requesting such information to the unit in custody of it. Lesotho authorities reported that information was directly accessible within the LRA in respect to one of the EOI requests received over the review period.

219. When the requested information is in the hands of other governmental agency, the taxpayer or a third party, the Investigations Section prepares a letter requesting the information in accordance to section 171 of the Income Tax Code. The timeline within which the information is to be provided is indicated in the letter. The Investigations Section reported that governmental agencies, taxpayers and third parties are usually given 7 days to provide the information but may request an extension when substantiated.

220. With the newly implemented EOI Manual, information that is readily available will be gathered by the official from the ITD Section who is handling the request. Information that needs to be sought from another governmental agency, the taxpayer or a third party would be forwarded by the ITD Section to the Operations Department. This is done through the use of a model template in which the information requested is specified for the Operations Department to gather. The Operations Department does not have access to the EOI request.

221. Where a search and seizure is require, LRA would engage the assistance of the national police, who will be the responsible of applying the search warrants to obtain the information. Search and seizure has never been used for exchange of information purposes.

222. Over the review period, the tax administration exercised these access powers with respect to one request. The information sought was banking information and a property lease agreement and the Investigations Section faced no practical difficulties in obtaining the information.

Use of information gathering measures absent domestic tax interest (ToR B.1.3)

223. The concept of "domestic tax interest" describes a situation where a contracting party can obtain and provide information to another contracting party only if it has an interest in the requested information for its own tax purposes.

224. The Income Tax Act provides the Commissioner General wide powers to directly obtain information from any person and is not restricted to information required for domestic purposes (s. 171).

225. Lesotho authorities and feedback from peers indicate that no difficulties have arisen in practice with obtaining or providing information requested by foreign competent authorities under EOI arrangements, irrespective of whether Lesotho needed the information for its own purposes.

Compulsory powers (ToR B.1.4)

226. Jurisdictions should have in place effective enforcement provisions to compel the production of information. There are administrative and criminal sanctions available to the Commissioner General in case of non-compliance with the obligation to provide the requested information.

227. As indicated under B.1.1, the Commissioner General can summon any person to provide the information and/or to be examined under oath to provide evidence regarding the tax affairs of that person or of any other person, as well as produce any book, record, or computer-stored information in their control (s. 171, ITA). Failure by these persons to co-operate with the Commissioner General would result in a penalty fine of LSL 5 000 (EUR 286) and/or imprisonment of up to six months (s. 182, 183, ITA).

228. Whilst the law does not require a search warrant, Lesotho authorities indicate that, in practice, the Lesotho Revenue Authority applies for such where the search for information covers residential premises of any person. This practice was adopted after referencing case law in South Africa[6], and to ensure that Lesotho authorities do not encounter any resistance by the persons holding the information who may cite constitutional rights. The Lesotho Constitution permits any search or seizure if it is necessary in a practical sense in a democratic society (s. 10(3)). To pre-empt any challenge on its powers provided in the Income Tax Act (s. 170), the Lesotho Revenue Authority has taken a deliberate policy decision that a search warrant would be obtained to carry out searches. Lesotho authorities are in the process of preparing draft legislation to amend the Income Tax Act to be in line with the Constitution. Over the review period, there were no cases in which the search for information covered residential premises thus requiring a search warrant. Further, the competent authority encountered no cases where a person who was required to keep information and/or has possession or control of the requested information challenged the obligation to furnish the information. In view of the limited practical experience over the review period, Lesotho should monitor the effectiveness of its powers to compel the production of information.

6. Cases in South Africa followed the Canadian approach where in Hunter v Southam Inc [1984] 2 S.C.R 145, the Court held that prior authorisation by an impartial and neutral person who is able to assess the evidence as to whether there is cause for the search in an objective manner is a necessary requirement for any search and seizure to be reasonable in a free and democratic society.

Secrecy provisions (ToR B.1.5)

229. Jurisdictions should not decline on the basis of secrecy provisions (e.g. bank secrecy, corporate secrecy) to respond to a request for information made pursuant to an exchange of information mechanism.

Bank secrecy

230. Lesotho's law provides for bank secrecy in respect of all information of "non-public nature" including that of any banks' clients (s. 29, FI Act), which may be interpreted to include information concerning the identity, accounts, deposits and transactions of banks' clients. Contravention of this section carries with it a fine of LSL 40 000 (EUR 2 287) and/or imprisonment of two years (s. 29(3)). A general penalty not exceeding LSL 500 000 (EUR 28 585) and an additional daily penalty of not less than LSL 5 000 (EUR 286) for a continuing offence, may also apply for any contravention of the provisions of the FI Act (s. 40). Notwithstanding, the exception when such protected information can be provided is when "lawfully required to do so… under the provision of any Act" (s. 29(1)).

231. In view of the exceptions to the bank secrecy provisions under the FI Act (s. 29(1)), the Lesotho authorities have confirmed that the competent authority, the Commissioner General of the LRA, can access all protected information since its access powers under the ITA imposes the obligation on all persons, including banks, to produce the required information upon receipt of the notice from the Commissioner General (as discussed in sections B.1.1 and B.1.2 above).

232. No issue with regard to the access of banking information have been reported by peers or experienced by Lesotho.

Professional privilege

233. The international standard allows the requested jurisdiction to decline to disclose information that constitutes confidential communication between a client and his/her admitted legal representative for the purpose of providing legal advice or for the purposes of existing or contemplated legal proceedings. This means that the protected information *(i)* should not be meant to be disclosed to any third persons, *(ii)* must have been obtained by the legal representative only when acting as a legal representative (and not in his/her other capacity such as a nominee shareholder, a trustee, a settlor, a company director or under a power of attorney to represent the company in its business affairs) and *(iii)* does not include purely factual information such as the identity of a director or beneficial owner of a company.

234. The Legal Practitioners Act of 1983 and the Accountants Act of 1977 govern legal professionals (which include lawyers, notaries and conveyancers) and accountants in the Kingdom of Lesotho, respectively. These laws are silent on client privileges and duties of confidentiality. The general common law principle applies where a person cannot be required to provide information or produce documents to which a claim to privilege could be maintained in legal proceedings. This principle is also incorporated in the MLPC Act that preserves the common law privilege of communication between a legal practitioner and a client concerning communication made in confidence between them for purposes of legal advice or litigation that is contemplated or has commenced.

235. Tax laws do not impose any restriction on the powers of the Commissioner General to obtain information from any of the legal professionals or accountants, and the Lesotho authorities state that it can obtain information from lawyers when they are not acting in their professional capacity. There is no case law in Lesotho on this issue but as Lesotho's legal system takes reference from South African case law, it should be noted that South Africa recognises the common law principle of legal professional privilege as a just cause to refuse to comply with a request to produce information to the tax authorities.[7] There are four essential requirements that have to be met before legal professional privilege may be successfully claimed:[8]

- the communications that are sought to be protected must have been made to a legal adviser acting in a professional capacity;
- the information must have been supplied in confidence;
- the information must have been supplied for the purpose of pending litigation or for the purpose of obtaining legal advice; and
- the client must claim the privilege.

236. These requirements are in accordance with the international standard. Case law shows that the mere fact that an attorney is in possession of confidential information does not create a legal professional privilege, as the attorney was not consulted to obtain legal advice.[9] Privilege is also not extended to other professional relationship, such as journalists, insurers, and doctors.[10]

7. As analysed by the Global Forum in the peer review report on South Africa.
8. Schwikkard and Van der Merwe, *Law of Evidence* (2009) at 135-6.
9. R v Davies 1956 (3) SA 52 (A).
10. S v Cornelissen 1994 (2) SACR 41 (W); Howe v Mabuya 1961 (2) SA 635 (D); Botha v Botha 1972 (2) SA 559 (N).

237. No peers indicated that professional secrecy has ever caused an issue in practice. There have been no cases in which and EOI request has been denied, or in which, as a result of the information provided, an entity or individual has raised and objection founded on professional secrecy.

Conclusion

238. The Lesotho competent authority has broad access powers to obtain and provide requested information held by persons within its territorial jurisdiction. All information gathering powers which can be used for domestic purposes can be used for EOI purposes regardless whether there is a domestic tax interest. Lesotho has in place enforcement provisions to compel the production of information, including criminal sanctions and search and seizure powers. Professional privilege under common law protects communication produced for purposes of seeking or providing legal advice or use in existing or contemplated legal proceedings.

Determination and factors underlying recommendations

Phase 1 determination
The element is in place.

Phase 2 Rating
Compliant

B.2. Notification requirements and rights and safeguards

> The rights and safeguards (e.g. notification, appeal rights) that apply to persons in the requested jurisdiction should be compatible with effective exchange of information.

Not unduly prevent or delay exchange of information (ToR B.2.1)

239. Rights and safeguards should not unduly prevent or delay effective exchange of information. For instance, notification rules should permit exceptions from notification of the taxpayer concerned prior to the exchange of information requested (e.g. in cases in which the information request is of a very urgent nature or the notification is likely to undermine the chance of success of the investigation conducted by the requesting jurisdiction).

240. Lesotho's law does not require the tax authorities to notify taxpayers or third parties of an exchange of information request, or when the tax authority collects information from a third party to fulfil an exchange of information request. There are also no specific legal provisions allowing the taxpayer to appeal the exchange of information.

Determination and factors underlying recommendations

Phase 1 determination
The element is in place.

Phase 2 Rating
Compliant

C. Exchanging information

Overview

241. Jurisdictions generally cannot exchange information for tax purposes unless they have a legal basis or mechanism for doing so. In Lesotho, the legal authority to exchange information is derived from DTA and TIEAs. This section of the report examines whether Lesotho has a network of information exchange that would allow it to achieve effective exchange of information in practice.

242. Lesotho has in total 14 EOI relationships through 7 bilateral agreements – 5 DTAs, 2 TIEAs, and with 7 other partners through the AMATM and the SADC Agreement. Regarding these multilateral agreements, there are 5 EOI relationships based solely on the SADC Agreement, 1 EOI relationship based solely on the AMATM and 1 EOI relationship based on both the SADC Agreement and AMATM. All DTAs and TIEAs are in force except for 2 DTAs with Botswana, and Seychelles, one of which is ready for signature and the other pending Cabinet approval to sign the re-negotiated version. Lesotho has deposited its instrument of ratification in respect of the AMATM and SADC Agreement, which are not yet in force, as they both first require a specific threshold number of member states of the African Tax Administration Forum and the South African Development Community to have ratified the agreement. Most of Lesotho's EOI mechanisms are in line with the standard, including the earlier signed DTA with Botswana, but not the earlier signed DTA with Seychelles which has been re-negotiated and is currently awaiting Cabinet approval for signature. Lesotho should ensure it expeditiously ratifies all EOI agreements and brings the DTA with the Seychelles to the standard.

243. Lesotho's EOI network covers all of its relevant partners. Nevertheless, Lesotho should continue its programme of updating its older agreements and entering into new agreements with all relevant partners, meaning those partners who expressed interest in entering into an EOI arrangement with Lesotho. During the course of the assessment, no jurisdiction advised that Lesotho had refused to enter into negotiations or conclude an EOI agreement.

244. All of Lesotho's EOI agreements have confidentiality provisions to ensure that the information exchanged will be disclosed only to persons authorised by the agreements. Effective measures and procedures have been put in place to ensure confidentiality of information received and exchanged, and to date, no issues with confidentiality as it relates to EOI requests have been reported by peers or experienced by Lesotho.

245. All EOI agreements also ensure that the contracting parties are not obliged to provide information which is subject to legal professional privilege. The term "professional secret" is not defined in the EOI agreements but as described under B.1.5, professional privilege in Lesotho is covered under common law, which is in line with the standard. Lesotho authorities have confirmed that professional privilege has never prevented tax authorities from accessing information requested for EOI purposes.

246. The Commissioner General of the LRA is designated as the competent authority for EOI purposes. Powers, duties and functions in relation to exchange of information and mutual agreement procedures contemplated in a tax treaty have been duly delegated into the person being the Manager of the ITD Section. There are no specific legal or regulatory requirements in place that would prevent Lesotho from responding to a request for information by providing the information requested or providing a status update within 90 days of receipt of the request. During the period under review (1 July 2012 – 30 June 2015) Lesotho received two requests from one jurisdiction. Although the number is limited, the EOI requests covered a range of ownership, accounting, banking and property information. Lesotho has provided information in one case within 90 days and in the other case within 180 days. Some delays have been identified when requests reach Lesotho's competent authority. As Lesotho presently only receives requests in hard copies Lesotho has contacted its current EOI partners to inform them on the most appropriate way to send EOI requests.

247. The procedures in place to handle EOI requests seem to be sufficient to handle incoming EOI requests, including the newly implemented EOI Manual indicating each of the steps involved in the handling of the EOI requests. The resources currently allocated to the ITD Section are adequate to deal with the present workload. Lesotho should continue to monitor the practical implementation of the organisational processes of the EOI unit, in particular taking account of any significant changes to the volume of incoming EOI requests, to ensure that they are sufficient for effective EOI in practice.

C.1. Exchange of information mechanisms

Exchange of information mechanisms should allow for effective exchange of information.

248. The international agreements providing for EOI have to be signed by the Minister of Finance, ratified by the Minister of Foreign Affairs and then tabled before Parliament in order to enter into force. Where any ratified international agreement conflicts with domestic law, the terms of the international agreement prevails over domestic law (s. 112, ITA Explanatory Memorandum).

249. Lesotho has in total 14 EOI relationships. These relationships are based on nine signed agreements – five DTAs, two TIEAs, AMATM and SADC Agreement. Of these, three DTAs and two TIEAs are in force. Lesotho has completed all domestic procedures to ratify all agreements except for two DTAs, one which has been re-negotiated and ready for signature and one in the process of obtaining Cabinet approval required to sign the re-negotiated version. Lesotho expects to sign the agreement that already has Cabinet approval in the fourth quarter of 2016.

250. Lesotho signed the AMATM and the SADC Agreement on 15 May 2014 and 18 August 2012 respectively. Lesotho has ratified these two agreements and deposited the instruments of ratification but these agreements are not yet in force as each first requires a specific threshold number of the respective member states of the African Tax Administration Forum and the South African Development Community to have ratified the agreement. The AMATM requires five member states and the SADC Agreement requires two thirds of the SADC member states. There are now five AMATM member states that have ratified the agreement. However, one has yet to deposit the ratification instrument. The AMATM will enter into force 30 days after the fifth member state deposits the ratification instrument.

251. The Lesotho authorities have an ongoing programme of concluding new EOI agreements and revising agreements where necessary in order to bring them up to standard. The older DTA in force with the United Kingdom was re-negotiated in 2014 and Lesotho recently obtained Cabinet approval for signature. Two other DTAs, while signed earlier in 2010 and 2011, were not ratified. The agreement with Botswana, which was in line with the standard, was updated in December 2014. The agreement with Seychelles has been re-negotiated to include text mirroring the OECD Model Convention and to ensure it is clearly in line with the international standard. Cabinet approval was obtained for signing the DTAs with Botswana, Malawi and Swaziland. Signature of these agreements is expected to take place in the fourth quarter of 2016.

Foreseeably relevant standard (ToR C.1.1)

252. The international standard for exchange of information envisages information exchange upon request to the widest possible extent, but does not allow "fishing expeditions," i.e. speculative requests for information that have no apparent nexus to an open inquiry or investigation. The balance between these two competing considerations is captured in the standard of "foreseeable relevance" which is included in Article 26(1) of the OECD Model Tax Convention and Article 1 of the OECD Model TIEA.

> The competent authorities of the contracting states shall exchange such information as is foreseeably relevant to the carrying out the provisions of this Convention or to the administration or enforcement of the domestic laws concerning taxes of every kind and description imposed on behalf of the contracting states or their political subdivisions or local authorities in so far as the taxation thereunder is not contrary to the Convention. The exchange of information is not restricted by Articles 1 and 2.

253. All of Lesotho's DTAs and TIEAs provide for exchange of information that is "foreseeably relevant" or "necessary" to the administration and enforcement of the domestic laws of the contracting parties concerning taxes covered in the DTAs. This scope is set out in the EOI Article in the relevant DTAs and is consistent with the international standard.[11]

254. The 1997 Lesotho-United Kingdom DTA and the 1997 Lesotho-Mauritius DTA provide for EOI as is necessary for carrying out the provisions of the Convention and "…in particular" to prevent fraud or evasion/legal avoidance. This scope has been interpreted by Lesotho as being wide enough to allow for EOI in line with the "foreseeably relevant" standard. The wording in the 1995 Lesotho-South Africa DTA as regards "foreseeably relevant" is in line with the standard. Notwithstanding, as these DTAs were signed before 2000 and therefore contain old text, Lesotho renegotiated all three DTAs to reflect language that is clearly in line with the international standard. However, these agreements have not yet been signed. Lesotho has reported that Cabinet approval was obtained to sign the renegotiated agreement with the United Kingdom but still pending for the agreement with Mauritius. The DTA between Lesotho and South Africa was signed on 18 September 2014 and entered into force on 27 May 2016.

11. The OECD Model Tax Convention on Income and on Capital recognises in its commentary to Article 26 (Exchange of Information) that the terms "necessary" and "relevant" allow the same scope of exchange of information as does the term "foreseeably relevant".

255. The Protocol amending the DTA with Seychelles, which was signed on the same date as the DTA, contains in paragraph 6 a provision that bank records will be exchanged only if the request identifies both a specific taxpayer and a specific bank. This provision is not in line with Article 26 of the OECD Model Tax Convention. Lesotho and Seychelles have since agreed to replace the Protocol with a version of Article 26 that mirrors that of the OECD Model Tax Convention that would therefore bring the DTA in line with the international standard. Negotiations of the revised Protocol that meets the international standard have been finalised and Lesotho is currently awaiting Cabinet approval for signature to take place.

256. The TIEAs with both the Bailiwick of Guernsey (Guernsey) and the Isle of Man, include qualifying language that the requested jurisdiction shall use "at its own discretion" all relevant information gathering measures "necessary" to provide the information requested. Lesotho authorities have confirmed that this slight deviation from the text in the OECD Model TIEA is aligned with the international standard.

257. Article 1 of the TIEAs with Guernsey and the Isle of Man contain a deviation from the OECD Model TIEA where the TIEAs provide that the requested party is not obliged "to provide information which is neither held by its authorities nor in the possession of or obtainable by persons who are within its territorial jurisdiction". These provisions use the words "obtainable by" instead of the expression "in control of" used in Article 2 of the OECD Model TIEA. The Lesotho authorities consider that the term "obtainable by" does not reduce EOI and actually may widen its effectiveness. This interpretation is also consistent with that of Guernsey's as noted in Guernsey's peer review report. This issue remains untested in practice as Lesotho has not exchanged information with Guernsey.

258. Under the TIEAs with Guernsey and the Isle of Man, the requesting jurisdiction has to provide, in addition to the requirements for a request set out in Article 5(5) of the OECD Model TIEA:

- "the reasons for believing that the information requested is foreseeably relevant to tax administration and enforcement of the requesting Party, with respect to the person identified in subparagraph (a) of this paragraph"; and
- "the period for which the information is requested".

259. Further, under the TIEA with Guernsey, it is not explicitly indicated that the purpose of the list of items that has to be included in the EOI request is to demonstrate foreseeable relevance. It does not appear that this exclusion or the above additional requirements may be inconsistent with the international standard. This issue remains untested in practice as Lesotho has not exchanged information with Guernsey.

Conclusion

260. Despite some deviations from the text in the OECD Model Tax Convention and TIEA, six of the seven DTAs and TIEAs signed by Lesotho are in line with the standard with regard to the foreseeable relevance standard. The DTA with the Seychelles is not in line with the international standard. Lesotho and the Seychelles have concluded the negotiations of a revised Protocol that meets the international standard. Lesotho is recommended to bring expeditiously all of its exchange of information arrangements in line with the standard.

261. Lesotho's EOI Manual, issued 28 July 2016 does not provide an explicit definition of foreseeable relevance. However, the EOI Manual does indicate that the process to handle an EOI request starts when a request is received from a treaty partner with the view to exchange information that is foreseeably relevant. Lesotho has reported that foreseeable relevance is interpreted in accordance to each of the EOI arrangements. In practice, Lesotho has never declined an EOI request on the basis of lack of foreseeable relevance.

In respect of all persons *(ToR C.1.2)*

262. For exchange of information to be effective it is necessary that a jurisdiction's obligation to provide information is not restricted by the residence or nationality of the person to whom the information relates or by the residence or nationality of the person in possession or control of the information requested. For this reason, the international standard envisages that exchange of information mechanisms will provide for exchange of information in respect of all persons.

263. All of Lesotho's five DTAs except the DTA with the United Kingdom explicitly provide that the EOI provision is not restricted by Article 1 (Persons Covered). However, as the domestic laws are applicable to non-residents as well as to residents, Lesotho has advised that it interprets the EOI provision to allow exchange of information with respect to all persons. Lesotho has also confirmed that the updated text of the Lesotho-United Kingdom DTA, which has been concluded and initialled on 6 February 2014, mirrors that of the OECD Model Tax Convention where the EOI provision is explicitly not restricted by Article 1, therefore eliminating any ambiguity that EOI between Lesotho and the United Kingdom is not in respect of all persons.

264. In respect of the two TIEAs signed by Lesotho, they contain the same provision to Article 2 of the OECD Model TIEA. The AMATM and SADC Agreement both provide for exchange of information in respect of all persons.

265. In practice, both discussions with the Lesotho authorities and feedback from peers, indicate that no difficulties have arisen with any of its EOI

partners regarding an EOI request relating to residents of either contracting states or residents of third party jurisdictions.

Obligation to exchange all types of information (ToR C.1.3)

266. Jurisdictions cannot engage in effective exchange of information if they cannot exchange information held by financial institutions, nominees or persons acting in an agency or a fiduciary capacity. The OECD Model Tax Convention and the Model TIEA, which are authoritative sources of the standards, stipulate that bank secrecy cannot form the basis for declining a request to provide information and that a request for information cannot be declined solely because the information is held by nominees or persons acting in an agency or fiduciary capacity or because the information relates to an ownership interest.

267. Out of Lesotho's five DTAs:

- The DTAs with Botswana, Mauritius, South Africa and the United Kingdom do not contain language akin to the Article 26(5) of the OECD Model Tax Convention providing for the obligations of the contracting parties to exchange information held by financial institutions, nominees, agents and ownership and identity information;
- The DTA with Seychelles contain language akin to Article 26(5) of the OECD Model Tax Convention;
- None of the DTAs signed by Lesotho prohibits exchange of information held by banks, nominees or persons acting in an agency or fiduciary capacity or because the information relates to an ownership interest.

268. For the four DTAs that do not contain language akin to Article 26(5) of the OECD Model Tax Convention, the absence of this language does not automatically create restrictions on exchange of bank information. The commentary to Article 26(5) indicates that while paragraph 5, added to the Model Tax Convention in 2005, represents a change in the structure of the Article, it should not be interpreted as suggesting that the previous version of the Article did not authorise the exchange of such information.

269. As neither Lesotho nor the four DTA partners[12] have domestic law limitations on access to bank information, the presence or absence in those agreements of a provision in line with Article 26(5) of the OECD Model Tax

12. Botswana, Mauritius, South Africa and the United Kingdom have been reviewed by the Global Forum and none of them have a domestic law limitation on access to bank information.

Convention does not result in them being inconsistent with the international standard for EOI.

270. Both TIEAs, AMATM and the SADC Agreement concluded by Lesotho contain a provision similar to Article 5(4) of the OECD Model TIEA, which ensures that the requested jurisdiction shall not decline to supply the information requested solely because it is held by a financial institution, nominee or person acting in an agency or a fiduciary capacity, or because it relates to ownership interests in a person.

271. Over the review period, Lesotho has exchanged ownership, accounting and banking information where it was requested.

Absence of domestic tax interest (ToR C.1.4)

272. The concept of "domestic tax interest" describes a situation where a requested jurisdiction can only provide information to a requesting jurisdiction if it has an interest in the requested information for its own tax purposes. An inability to provide information based on a domestic tax interest requirement is not consistent with the international standard. Requested jurisdictions must use their information gathering measures even though invoked solely to obtain and provide information to the requesting jurisdiction.

273. Out of Lesotho's five DTAs:

- The DTAs with Botswana, Mauritius, South Africa and the United Kingdom do not contain provisions similar to Article 26(4) of the OECD Model Tax Convention, which oblige the contracting parties to use their information gathering measures to obtain and provide information to the requesting jurisdiction even in cases where the requested party does not have a domestic interest in the requested information;
- The DTA with Seychelles contains language akin to Article 26(4) of the OECD Model Tax Convention.

274. There are no domestic tax interest restrictions on Lesotho's powers to access information for EOI purposes (see Section B above). As such, the exchange of information in the absence of domestic interest in respect of the four DTAs will be subject to reciprocity and will depend on the domestic limitations (if any) in the laws of some of these partners. As neither Lesotho nor any of the four DTA partners require a domestic tax interest in order to exchange information[13], the presence or absence in those agreements of a

13. Botswana, Mauritius, South Africa and the United Kingdom have been reviewed by the Global Forum and none of them require a domestic tax interest to exchange information.

provision in line with Article 26(4) of the OECD Model Tax Convention does not result in them being inconsistent with the international standard for EOI.

275. In practice, officials from Lesotho, and feedback from peers confirms, that in all cases Lesotho has provided information to the requesting jurisdiction regardless of whether or not Lesotho has an interest in the requested information for its own tax purposes.

Absence of dual criminality principles (ToR C.1.5)

276. The principle of dual criminality provides that assistance can only be provided if the conduct being investigated (and giving rise to an information request) would constitute a crime under the laws of the requested jurisdiction if it had occurred in the requested jurisdiction. In order to be effective, exchange of information should not be constrained by the application of the dual criminality principle.

277. There are no such limiting provisions in any of Lesotho's EOI instruments which would indicate that there is dual criminality principle to be applied.

278. The process for exchanging information related to criminal matters is the same as that for civil matters. In practice, Lesotho has only exchanged information for civil matters.

Exchange of information in both civil and criminal tax matters (ToR C.1.6)

279. Information exchange may be requested both for tax administration purposes and for tax prosecution purposes. The international standard is not limited to information exchange in criminal tax matters but extends to information requested for tax administration purposes (also referred to as "civil tax matters").

280. All of Lesotho's EOI instruments provide for exchange of information in both civil and criminal tax matters.

281. The process for exchanging information related to criminal matters is the same as for civil matters. In practice, Lesotho has only exchanged information for civil matters.

Provide information in specific form requested (ToR C.1.7)

282. In some cases, a contracting party may need to receive information in a particular form to satisfy its evidentiary or other legal requirements. Such formats may include depositions of witnesses and authenticated copies of original records. Contracting parties should endeavour as far as possible to accommodate such requests. The requested party may decline to provide the

information in the specific form requested if, for instance, the requested form is not known or permitted under its law administrative practice. A refusal to provide the information in the form requested does not affect the obligation to provide the information.

283. All of Lesotho's EOI instruments do not restrict the provision of information in specific form requested (including depositions of witnesses and production of authenticated copies of original documents) to the extent allowable under Lesotho's domestic laws.

284. Neither of the requests Lesotho received during the review period were requested in a specific format.

In force (ToR C.1.8)

285. Exchange of information cannot take place unless a jurisdiction has exchange of information arrangements in force. The international standard requires that jurisdictions must take all steps necessary to bring agreements that have been signed into force expeditiously.

286. As regards concluding and ratification of treaties, Lesotho authorities have advised that Lesotho takes guidance from the British Constitution procedure which involves the exercise of the Royal Prerogative Power. The following practice that is described is laid out in a "Treaty-Making Practice" which is adhered to by all government authorities. This aspect of common law has been inherited by Lesotho and by implication, the negotiation, signing and ratification or accession to treaties is considered "executive acts". With respect to EOI agreements, after the draft agreement has been concluded between Lesotho and a foreign government, the Ministry of Finance prepares a cabinet memorandum seeking approval from the Cabinet to sign the agreement. Once the agreement is signed, approval is thereafter sought from the sovereign, in whom the "executive authority" is vested as per the Constitution of the Kingdom of Lesotho (s. 86) to ratify the agreement. Once the sovereign approves, the "Instrument of Ratification" is issued and the EOI agreement is considered ratified. Before the EOI agreement enters into force in Lesotho, it must be "domesticated" by an Act of Parliament. Lesotho authorities have advised that in order to shorten the process by which the treaty would have to be debated in parliament in the form of a Bill, the Lesotho Cabinet has taken a decision that all treaties would be tabled before Parliament for "notice and information only". This process gives the Parliament an opportunity to highlight any relevant considerations before the EOI agreement enters into force in Lesotho. Following this parliamentary process, the EOI agreement is considered ready to enter into force in Lesotho. The "domestication process" then commences with publishing a Legal Notice to inform the general public of Lesotho about the new EOI agreement and the date on which it enters into force.

287. Five of Lesotho's seven bilateral EOI agreements are in force. These are the three older DTAs with Mauritius, South Africa and the United Kingdom, all of which have been re-negotiated in 2014 and awaiting finalisation or signature. Lesotho has reported that Cabinet approval was obtained to sign the DTA renegotiated with United Kingdom and are expected to sign in the fourth quarter of 2016. The two TIEAs with Guernsey and the Isle of Man were signed in July and September 2013, respectively, and entered into force on 3 January 2015.The two DTAs that are not in force are with Botswana and Seychelles. While signed earlier in 2010 and 2011, these agreements were not brought into force as they were further updated in December 2014 with text mirroring the OECD Model Convention and to ensure it is clearly in line with the international standard. Lesotho informed that the re-negotiation of the DTA with Seychelles was finalised and Lesotho is currently awaiting Cabinet approval for signature. The DTA signed with Botswana already obtained Cabinet approval and Lesotho is expected to sign in the fourth quarter of 2016. The earlier signed agreements with Mauritius, South Africa, United Kingdom and Botswana are in line with the standard.

288. Lesotho authorities have advised that some delays are encountered in signing and ratifying of agreements due to administrative constraints in Lesotho which involves different offices within the government relaying responsibilities and awaiting feedback. Lesotho is recommended to ensure it ratifies and bring into force its EOI agreements as quickly as possible. Lesotho authorities are recommended to take the necessary steps to effectively monitor the ratification process for signed conventions in order to ensure that the process is completed expeditiously.

289. The AMATM and SADC Agreement, while both signed and ratified by Lesotho, have not entered into force as they require a specific threshold of member states of the African Tax Administration Forum and the South African Development Community to have ratified before the agreements can enter into force. The AMATM requires five member states and the SADC Agreement requires two thirds of the SADC member states. There are now five AMATM member states that have ratified the agreement. However, one has yet to deposit the ratification instrument. The AMATM will enter into force 30 days after the fifth member state deposits the ratification instrument.

Be given effect through domestic law (ToR C.1.9)

290. For exchange of information to be effective, the contracting parties must enact any legislation necessary to comply with the terms of the agreement.

291. As discussed in section B, Lesotho has the legislative and regulatory framework in place to give effect to its agreements.

Determination and factors underlying recommendations

Phase 1 determination
The element is in place.

Phase 2 Rating
Compliant

C.2. Exchange of information mechanisms with all relevant partners

The jurisdictions' network of information exchange mechanisms should cover all relevant partners.

292. Ultimately, the international standard requires that jurisdictions exchange information with all relevant partners, meaning those partners who are interested in entering into an information exchange arrangement. Agreements cannot be concluded only with counterparties without economic significance. If it appears that a jurisdiction is refusing to enter into agreements or negotiations with partners, in particular ones that have a reasonable expectation of requiring information from that jurisdiction in order to properly administer and enforce its tax laws it may indicate a lack of commitment to implement the standards.

293. Lesotho has an EOI network covering 14jurisdictions through five DTAs, two TIEAs, the AMATM and SADC Agreement that also provide for the exchange of information. Lesotho's EOI network covers significant partners, including South Africa – its most significant trading partner; and several jurisdictions in the region through the AMATM and SADC Agreement.

294. Ultimately, the international standard requires jurisdictions to exchange information with their relevant partners, meaning those partners who are interested in entering into an exchange of information agreement. During the course of the assessment, no jurisdiction has advised that Lesotho had refused to enter into negotiations or conclude an EOI agreement.

295. Lesotho has in place an on-going negotiation programme that includes plans for renegotiation of older EOI agreements to update the text to be consistent with the OECD Model Tax Convention. Lesotho has also advised that it has recently further concluded DTA negotiations with regional partners such as Malawi and Swaziland. Cabinet approval was obtained for both agreements and Lesotho has reported that they are expected to sign in

the fourth quarter of 2016. Negotiations are also underway with Malaysia. In addition, Lesotho has also signed on to the two multilateral agreements – AMATM and SADC Agreement, which after it enters into force, will enable Lesotho to exchange with a larger number of jurisdictions in its region.

296. Moreover, Lesotho has informed that the officials from LRA have prepared a motivation which has been presented to the Minister of Finance for approval to sign the Multilateral Convention on Mutual Administrative Assistance in Tax Matters, as amended (Multilateral Convention). Upon approval from the Minister Lesotho will request to be invited to join the Multilateral Convention.

Determination and factors underlying recommendations

Phase 1 determination	
The element is in place.	
Factors underlying recommendations	**Recommendations**
	Lesotho should continue to develop its EOI network to the standard with all relevant partners.

Phase 2 Rating
Compliant

C.3. Confidentiality

> The jurisdictions' mechanisms for exchange of information should have adequate provisions to ensure the confidentiality of information received.

Information received: disclosure, use, and safeguards (ToR C.3.1)

297. Governments would not engage in information exchange without the assurance that the information provided would only be used for the purposes permitted under the exchange mechanism and that its confidentiality would be preserved. Information exchange instruments must therefore contain confidentiality provisions that spell out specifically to whom the information can be disclosed and the purposes for which the information can be used. In addition to the protections afforded by the confidentiality provisions of information exchange instruments, jurisdictions with tax systems generally impose strict confidentiality requirements on information collected for tax purposes.

International treaties

298. All of Lesotho's EOI agreements have confidentiality provisions to ensure that the information exchanged will be disclosed only to persons authorised by the agreements.

299. While the articles in Lesotho's DTAs may vary slightly in wording, these provisions contain all of the essential aspects of Article 26(2) of the OECD Model Tax Convention. Only the DTA with the United Kingdom does not refer to the confidentiality provision of the domestic laws of the Contracting States. In the case of Lesotho, this does not prevent the enforcement of the confidentiality duty since information received from partner jurisdictions are received on the basis of an international agreement signed in application of the Income Tax Act, and therefore the domestic provision assessed below will apply.

300. Both Lesotho's TIEAs have confidentiality provisions modelled on Article 8 of the OECD Model TIEA. Confidentiality of the provided information in line with the standard is also provided for in Article 8 of the AMATM and Article 8 of the SADC Agreement.

Lesotho's domestic law

301. Under Lesotho's Income Tax Act, all officers of the LRA must first take an oath of secrecy before taking up their duties at the tax administration. Through the oath of secrecy, officials agree and solemnly swear that they shall not divulge or disclose or be party to divulging or disclosing to any unauthorised person, any information, documentary or otherwise whatsoever, relating to the income, expenditure or other financial dealings or status of any taxpayer or other person involved in the operations in furtherance of the Lesotho Revenue Authority Act, and any confidential information including instructions, directives or orders in respect of the administration of the Act which may come to their possession, knowledge or attention, either in the course of their duties or in their capacity as an officer or staff member. Officers must also not communicate such information to any other person except in the performance of their duties under the Income Tax Act (s. 202(1)). Sanctions apply if there are offences related to secrecy and persons convicted are liable to a fine of up to LSL 5 000 (EUR 283) and/or imprisonment of up to six months (s. 186).

302. The Internal Affairs Unit (IAU) from the LRA monitors that secrecy provisions are respected by all LRA officials. As at April 2016, the IAU is comprised of ten officials: head, operational manager, four investigators, three ethics officials and one assistant. Part of the IAU's mandate deals with prevention, and this is done through integrity building initiatives handled by the ethics officials. These initiatives include ethics awareness campaigns that

are held regularly for staff and in which confidentiality and secrecy provisions are always addressed. There has never been a case in which an official was suspended for breach of confidentiality of improper or unauthorised disclosure of information.

303. The Income Tax Act permits the disclosure of information "when the competent authority of the government of a country with which an agreement for the avoidance of double taxation exists, to the extent permitted under that agreement" (s. 202(3)(c)). The conditions to permitting the disclosure of information to other competent authorities are deferred to the provisions in Lesotho's EOI agreements which would take full legal effect. This is in line with the international standard. Lesotho has reported that these provisions have never been applied in practice.

Confidentiality in practice

304. The LRA has internal measures in place to ensure that confidentiality practices are being respected by all officers concerned with the EOI process. These measures ensure that access to highly confidential information such as EOI requests is limited. Only three persons have access to each EOI request and the request responses. As such, access to confidential information is restricted to the Commissioner General who is the competent authority, the Manager of ITD and the Senior Official working within the ITD Section. The Manager of the Legal and Policy Division might also have access to confidential EOI information when acting as the ITD Manager supervisor. All controls, requests and responses recording systems are handled by the ITD Section.

305. The incoming and outgoing EOI requests and related documents are kept in the offices of the Manager of ITD. Only the Manager of ITD has a key to this office, except while on leave, in which case the key is left with the Senior Official within the International Treaty Section Unit. The ITD Section is in one of the LRA's buildings in Maseru and public is not authorised to enter this building. If for any reason there are visitors in the facilities, these would be accompanied at all times by LRA officials. Any visitor would need to register with proper identification.

306. Both staff members of the ITD Section have their own password-protected computer. A high quality copier, scanner and printer is available within the LRA building in which the ITD Section is located. Any printed document containing confidential information and which will not be kept within the EOI files is meant to be destroyed personally by the staff member in charge of the case.

307. All EOI requests are made or received through the competent authority. EOI requests received by the competent authority are marked

"confidential". Immediately a hard file is opened for each request and these are kept in the secure cabinet within the office of the ITD Manager's office.

308. When requesting information from other office within the LRA (e.g. operations division), only the minimum information contained in the request is disseminated and not the entire request. Further, these communications with other LRA offices are stamped with the confidentiality stamp which contains the following wording: "The information is furnished under the provisions of an International Tax Treaty with a foreign government – the use and disclosure must be governed by the provisions of that treaty". Officials from other offices in LRA are bound by the oath of secrecy they undertake, to keep information confidential.

309. In the course of gathering the requested information, communications with other offices used to be done through e-mail. However, as at 28 July 2016 when the EOI Manual was published, communications are being done in closed and sealed envelopes with the confidentiality stamp.

310. On providing the information to the EOI partner, responses are generally sent through registered mail, whereby a mail tracking function is in place. When the EOI partner so requests, Lesotho authorities may transmit the requested information electronically by using the encryption system or platform provided by the EOI partner.

All other information exchanged (ToR C.3.2)

311. The confidentiality provisions in Lesotho's exchange of information agreements and domestic law do not draw a distinction between information received in response to requests or information forming part of the requests themselves. As such, these provisions apply equally to all requests for such information, background documents to such requests, and any other document reflecting such information, including communications between the requesting and requested jurisdictions and communications within the tax authorities of either jurisdiction.

Conclusion

312. Feedback from peers indicates that there have been no issues with confidentiality regarding EOI requests to date. Lesotho authorities have confirmed that there have been no cases in which information received by the Competent Authority from the EOI partner has been made public or disclosed to a third party. Further, confidentiality is being reinforced with the new practices included in the EOI Manual.

Determination and factors underlying recommendations

Phase 1 determination
The element is in place.

Phase 2 Rating
Compliant

C.4. Rights and safeguards of taxpayers and third parties

The exchange of information mechanisms should respect the rights and safeguards of taxpayers and third parties.

Exceptions to requirement to provide information (ToR C.4.1)

313. The international standard allows requested parties not to supply information in response to a request in certain identified situations where an issue of trade, business or other secret may arise.

314. Communications between a client and an attorney or other admitted legal representative are only privileged to the extent that the attorney or other legal representative acts in his or her capacity as an attorney or other legal representative. Where legal professional privilege is more broadly defined it does not provide valid grounds on which to decline a request for EOI. To the extent, therefore, that an attorney acts in another capacity, such as a nominee shareholder, a trustee, a settlor, a company director, EOI resulting from and relating to any such activity cannot be declined because of legal professional privilege.

315. All of Lesotho's EOI agreements ensure that the contracting parties are not obliged to provide information which is subject to legal professional privilege. However, the term "professional secret" is not defined in the EOI agreements and therefore this term would derive its meaning from the Lesotho's domestic laws. As described in section B.1.5 of this report, professional privilege in Lesotho is covered under common law which protects communication produced for purposes of seeking or providing legal advice or use in existing or contemplated legal proceedings. There have not been any cases in which an EOI request has been denied or in which, an entity or individual has refused to provide information founded on professional secrecy.

316. The TIEAs with Guernsey and the Isle of Man contain a deviation where the applicability of the rights and safeguards secured to persons is detached from the conditionality that it is only to the extent that they do not unduly prevent or delay effective exchange of information. Instead, it is also indicated, in the following separate sentence that the requested jurisdiction

"shall use its best endeavours" to ensure that the effective exchange of information is not unduly prevented or delayed". Consequently, it is also noted that in Lesotho, Guernsey and the Isle of Man, the rights and safeguards that may be applicable are not expected to be obtrusive to effective exchange of information. It is thus unlikely that this variation will materially affect the exchange of information to the international standards. This issue remains untested in practice as Lesotho has not exchanged information with Guernsey or Isle of Man. Lesotho is therefore recommended to monitor that appropriate measures are in place to prevent that the application of rights and safeguards unduly prevent the effective exchange of information with Guernsey and Isle of Man.

Determination and factors underlying recommendations

Phase 1 determination
The element is in place.

Phase 2 Rating
Compliant

C.5. Timeliness of responses to requests for information

The jurisdiction should provide information under its network of agreements in a timely manner.

Responses within 90 days (ToR C.5.1)

317. In order for exchange of information to be effective, it needs to be provided in a timeframe which allows tax authorities to apply the information to the relevant cases. If a response is provided but only after a significant lapse of time, the information may no longer be of use to the requesting authorities. This is particularly important in the context of international co-operation as cases in this area must be of sufficient importance to warrant making a request.

318. None of Lesotho's DTAs, AMATM or SADC Agreement require the provision of request confirmations, status updates or the provision of the requested information within the timeframes foreshadowed in Article 5(6) of the OECD Model TIEA. The TIEAs with Guernsey and the Isle of Man require that the competent authority of the requested jurisdiction confirms receipt of a request within 30 days; notifies any deficiencies in the request within 60 days; and, if unable to obtain and provide the requested information within 90 days, immediately inform the requesting jurisdiction and explain the reason for its inability, the nature of the obstacles or the reasons for refusing to provide information (art. 4(6) of both TIEAs).

319. There are no specific legal or regulatory requirements in place that would prevent Lesotho from responding to a request for information by providing the information requested or providing a status update within 90 days of receipt of the request.

320. Over the three-year review period, from 1 July 2012 to 30 June 2015, Lesotho received two EOI requests from one jurisdiction which is Lesotho's most relevant trading partner. Although the number is limited, the EOI requests covered a wide range of information: financial statements, accounting records, tax return, banking information and property contracts.

321. Feedback from the peer indicates that they were generally satisfied with Lesotho's timeliness of response to EOI requests made during the review period. The time periods are calculated from the date of receipt of the request to the date on which final and complete response was received. In 50% of the cases (1 request), full information was provided within 90 days while in the other 50% of the cases (1 request) information was provided within 180 days. In this case however, the peer reported that partial information was provided within 90 days. The request that was answered within 180 days sought a range of different types of information which the competent authority obtained from different sources.

322. Peers have indicated that one of the requests, the one which for the purposes of this report is considered to have been responded within 180 days, was actually responded within 191 days. This however, obeys to the amount of time the request took to reach Lesotho's competent authority. Lesotho presently only receives requests in hard copies and depending on the means used, the delivery of the request, as in this case, might be delayed. Although Lesotho has updated information in the Global Forum's competent authority database, Lesotho has contacted its current EOI partners to inform them further on the most appropriate way to send EOI requests.

323. Lesotho has confirmed that any requests, irrespective of the number of persons/entities involved or pieces of information requested, is counted as a single request. It has not happened that additional information to a request is sought but in such a case, Lesotho reported that the further request would be regarded as a new single request.

324. Over the three-year period under review, Lesotho has never failed to obtain and provide information requested. In addition, Lesotho has never requested clarification from the requesting jurisdiction before providing the information.

Organisational process and resources (ToR C.5.2)

325. It is important that a jurisdiction has appropriate organisational processes and resources in place to ensure a timely response.

326. The competent authority for exchange of information purposes in Lesotho is the Commissioner General, who has delegated its functions as competent authority to the Manager of the ITD Section. The contact details of the competent authority are published in the Global Forum's competent authorities database and this information is kept up-to-date. These details are also provided to Lesotho's EOI partners, when they require confirmation or in case of any changes.

327. The ITD Section is responsible for implementing all EOI agreements, processing all EOI requests and maintaining a regular contact with Lesotho's partners, generally done by phone or e-mail. The Section consists of two staff members, i.e. Manager at degree level with five years supervisory experience and senior official also at degree level with a minimum of three years of experience in the field of accounting, taxation or law. The senior official joined very recently and started EOI training. The staff resources allocated to the ITD Section for the handling of EOI requests are set at the appropriate level considering the low number of requests and it is expected that this will continue as such in case the number of requests increases.

328. Every staff member in the ITD Section has his/her own computer. A high quality copier/scanner/printer is available within the premises in which the ITD Section is located but it is not for the exclusive use of the Section. A specific e-mail address was created for the competent authority and it is only accessible by the ITD Section manager.

329. Lesotho's competent authority has installed the EOI tracking system (case management system) developed by the Global Forum Secretariat and the World Bank Group to track and monitor the number of EOI cases and workflow. This system is installed in the computer of the ITD Section Manager. This system includes the date of the request's receipt, the requesting party reference number, the requested party internal reference number, the response sending date, among other relevant case details. It generates automatic alerts when certain deadlines are due.

330. There is not a specifically dedicated budget for EOI purposes due to the low volume of requests Lesotho has received so far; the budget allocated to the ITD Section covers all financial needs related to EOI. Lesotho has reported that for gathering the information, the Investigations Unit caters for the requests under its own recurring budget. Lesotho authorities have informed that they plan to set aside a dedicated budget line in the 2016-17 budget of approximately LSL 32 000 to cover for expenses related to the gathering of information and courier fees. The wages of the ITD Section officials in charge of handling EOI requests is not included here.

Handling of EOI requests

331. The EOI Manual issued by the Lesotho Revenue Authority in 28 July 2016 describes the steps required by its staff members in processing incoming and outgoing EOI requests.

332. All EOI requests are initially received by the competent authority, who by delegation is the ITD Section. The request can be received in the form of a letter from the Commissioner General's office or the Records Office, or through the EOI e-mail. The officer who receives the request must immediately update the EOI case management system.

333. The officer must acknowledge receipt within seven calendar days upon reception of the EOI request. The signed letter needs to be copied and stored in the case file kept by the competent authority and dispatched through any of the permitted channels, i.e. records management, courier services or secure e-mail transmission. The officer must again update the case management system. The competent authority has developed a template for purposes of confirming the reception of the EOI request.

334. Immediately after, the request must be reviewed to determine if it's valid. The ITD official uses a quality control template to determine if the exchange is based on a valid legal instrument and if the request adheres to EOI international standards. If the request is not valid, the ITD Manager will discuss the possible reasons for rejection with the Chief Legal Policy Officer and drafts the letter to reject the request using the template that has been created for this purpose. Where applicable, all relevant documentation will be stamped with the confidentiality stamp. If based on the initial review of the request the competent authority determines that clarification is required, a letter should be drafted using the template that has been created for this purpose.

335. When the request has been verified and considered valid, the official will proceed to gather the information. The first step will be for the officer of the ITD Section to determine whether the information is readily available within the LRA or not. If the information is readily available within the LRA, the official will gather the information making use of the LRA internal systems and will provide to the treaty partner within 90 days. If the information is not readily available within the LRA, and the information is to be sought outside of the LRA, the request will be allocated to the relevant operations division for them to gather the information. The competent authority has developed a template for those cases in which the information is required from an operations division to guard confidentiality. Before the EOI Manual entered into force in28 July 2016, the competent authority would ask the Investigations Unit to gather all information, notwithstanding if it was readily available in the LRA or not.

336. When information gathered by the operations division reaches the competent authority, the official in charge must determine whether the response is a partial response or a final full response. To do this, the official must compare the information requested by the EOI partner to that information collected. In case the information is not complete, the official should contact the responsible LRA official to obtain an explanation and, if needed, to instruct further to collect the correct information. If the information gathering powers have been exhausted and the information is incomplete due to a lack of response from the third party, the case should be referred to the Litigations Division for further consideration.

337. The official in the competent authority will proceed to compile the final response by completing all relevant sections of the full response template created for this purposes. If it is not possible to compile a final response, a partial response is to be provided using the partial response template. The response is then submitted to the ITD Section for review and approval. Where applicable, all relevant documentation is to be stamped with the confidentiality stamp. A copy of the final response is to be kept in the files of the competent authority. Once completed, the request is sent through registered mail. The response to the EOI request containing information that is not readily available within the LRA must be provided in 182 days.

338. The EOI Manual recently in force in Lesotho for the handling of EOI requests comprehends the steps necessary to validate the request, gather the information and compile the response. However, the EOI Manual does not refer to specific timelines that need to be followed for each of the steps and only includes references to 90 and 182 days depending on whether the information is readily available or not within the LRA. Further, the EOI Manual does not include any section in which an update is provided to the EOI partner where a response cannot be provided within the 90 days. It is recommended that the Lesotho competent authority includes specific timelines for the completion of each of the steps involved in processing the EOI request to ensure that the response will be provided within the timeframes set in the EOI Manual. Further, considering that the EOI Manual was not tested during the review period, Lesotho should monitor the practical implementation of the EOI Manual to ensure that EOI requests are dealt with effectively and efficiently.

339. Over the review period, Lesotho authorities informed that there have been no cases where an EOI partner had to make further enquiries in relation to information provided by Lesotho because the response was perceived as incomplete or inadequate. Feedback from peers confirms that they were generally satisfied with the level of co-operation shown by Lesotho.

Absence of unreasonable, disproportionate, or unduly restrictive conditions on exchange of information (ToR C.5.3)

340. Exchange of information assistance should not be subject to unreasonable, disproportionate, or unduly restrictive conditions. Other than those matters identified earlier in this report, there are no further conditions that appear to restrict effective exchange of information in Lesotho. There are no legal or regulatory requirements in Lesotho that impose unreasonable, disproportionate or unduly restrictive conditions.

Conclusion

341. The resources currently allocated to the ITD Section are adequate to deal with the present workload. The procedures established by the LRA as described in the EOI Manual seem to be sufficient to handle incoming requests.

342. Lesotho's practices to date have demonstrated a responsive approach. Lesotho responded to all of its EOI requests, one within 90 days and one within 180 days. Lesotho's EOI partners that have provided peer input indicated that progress update were provided where their request was not answered within 90 days. All in all, Lesotho's peers have generally been positive by the level of co-operation shown by Lesotho. Lesotho should continue to monitor the practical implementation of the organisational processes of the EOI unit, in particular taking account of any significant changes to the volume of incoming EOI requests, to ensure that they are sufficient for effective EOI in practice.

Determination and factors underlying recommendations

Phase 1 determination
The assessment team is not in a position to evaluate whether this element is in place, as it involves issues of practice that are dealt with in the Phase 2 review.

Phase 2 Rating	
Largely Compliant	
Factor underlying recommendation	**Recommendations**
Lesotho has allocated resources and has in place organisational processes for exchange of information that appear to be adequate for dealing with incoming EOI requests in a timely manner. Lesotho has only received 2 requests for information.	Lesotho should continue to monitor the practical implementation of the organisational processes of the EOI unit, in particular taking account of any significant changes to the volume of incoming EOI requests, to ensure that they are sufficient for effective EOI in practice.

Summary of determinations and factors underlying recommendations

Overall Rating
LARGELY COMPLIANT

Determination	Factors underlying recommendations	Recommendations
Jurisdictions should ensure that ownership and identity information for all relevant entities and arrangements is available to their competent authorities *(ToR A.1)*		
The element is in place but certain aspects of the legal implementation of the element need improvement.	While there are no share warrants to bearer in circulation at present, the mechanisms in place may be insufficient to ensure the availability of identity information all holders of share warrants.	Lesotho should take steps to ensure that robust mechanisms are in place to identify owners of share warrants to bearer or eliminate companies' ability to issue such share warrants.
Phase 2 Rating: Partially Compliant	Domestic and foreign (external) companies were not regularly monitored during the review period. However in December 2015 a programme was put in place to monitor compliance of the obligations in the Companies Act. As a result, 17 591 out of 29 030 companies were struck off from the Companies Registry and a new regular oversight programme was established to systematically monitor compliance with these obligations.	Lesotho should monitor the implementation of this new oversight programme and exercise its enforcement powers as appropriate to ensure that ownership and identity information for domestic and foreign (external) companies is available in practice.

Determination	Factors underlying recommendations	Recommendations
Phase 2 Rating: Partially Compliant *(continued)*	Lesotho authorities do not have regular oversight to monitor the compliance of legal obligations to ensure that ownership and identity information is available for general partnerships, all types of (including voting trusts) and societies. Existing enforcement provisions to ensure that ownerships and identity information is available for these type of entities or arrangements have never been applied in practice.	Lesotho should put in place an oversight programme to ensure compliance with the obligations to maintain ownership and identity information of partnerships, all types of trusts and societies, and exercise its enforcement powers as appropriate to ensure that such information is available in practice.
Jurisdictions should ensure that reliable accounting records are kept for all relevant entities and arrangements *(ToR A.2)*		
The element is in place, but certain aspects of the legal implementation of the element need improvement.	Only trusts that receive taxable income would be subject to obligations under the Income Tax Act to keep accounting records. The availability of accounting information is not ensured for trusts that receive only foreign-source income.	Lesotho should ensure the availability of accounting records of all trusts in Lesotho even where the trust is not carrying on business or is not subject to tax in Lesotho.
Phase 2 Rating: Largely Compliant	Lesotho authorities monitor compliance with the accounting recordkeeping obligations prescribed by the tax laws but this supervision is limited to registered taxpayers, which include domestic and foreign (external) companies, partnerships and trusts deriving income in Lesotho. There is a regular oversight programme which covers that the accounting requirements prescribed by the Income Tax Act are complied with. However, the compliance level for partnerships is low and trusts that only receive foreign-source income and where the settlor is a non-resident are not covered by the oversight that LRA conducts.	Lesotho should put in place a comprehensive oversight programme to ensure compliance with and enforcement of the obligation to maintain reliable accounting records and underlying documents for all relevant entities and arrangements.

Determination	Factors underlying recommendations	Recommendations
Banking information should be available for all account-holders *(ToR A.3)*		
The element is in place.		
Phase 2 Rating: Largely Compliant	During the review period there was no oversight on compliance of AML regulations by banks regarding their customer due diligence requirements.	Lesotho should put in place an oversight programme to ensure compliance with AML regulations and effectively apply enforcement measures on banks regarding their customer due diligence requirements.
Competent authorities should have the power to obtain and provide information that is the subject of a request under an exchange of information arrangement from any person within their territorial jurisdiction who is in possession or control of such information (irrespective of any legal obligation on such person to maintain the secrecy of the information *(ToR B.1)*		
The element is in place.		
Phase 2 Rating: Compliant		
The rights and safeguards (e.g. notification, appeal rights) that apply to persons in the requested jurisdiction should be compatible with effective exchange of information *(ToR B.2)*		
The element is in place.		
Phase 2 Rating: Compliant		
Exchange of information mechanisms should allow for effective exchange of information *(ToR C.1)*		
The element is in place.		
Phase 2 Rating: Compliant		
The jurisdictions' network of information exchange mechanisms should cover all relevant partners *(ToR C.2)*		
The element is in place.		Lesotho should continue to develop its EOI network to the standard with all relevant partners.

<table>
<tr><th>Determination</th><th>Factors underlying recommendations</th><th>Recommendations</th></tr>
<tr><td>Phase 2 Rating: Compliant</td><td></td><td></td></tr>
<tr><td colspan="3">The jurisdictions' mechanisms for exchange of information should have adequate provisions to ensure the confidentiality of information received (ToR C.3)</td></tr>
<tr><td>The element is in place.</td><td></td><td></td></tr>
<tr><td>Phase 2 Rating: Compliant</td><td></td><td></td></tr>
<tr><td colspan="3">The exchange of information mechanisms should respect the rights and safeguards of taxpayers and third parties (ToR C.4)</td></tr>
<tr><td>The element is in place.</td><td></td><td></td></tr>
<tr><td>Phase 2 Rating: Compliant</td><td></td><td></td></tr>
<tr><td colspan="3">The jurisdiction should provide information under its network of agreements in a timely manner (ToR C.5)</td></tr>
<tr><td>The assessment team is not in a position to evaluate whether this element is in place, as it involves issues of practice that are dealt with in the Phase 2 review.</td><td></td><td></td></tr>
<tr><td>Phase 2 Rating: Largely Compliant</td><td>Lesotho has allocated resources and has in place organisational processes for exchange of information that appear to be adequate for dealing with incoming EOI requests in a timely manner. Lesotho has only received 2 requests for information.</td><td>Lesotho should continue to monitor the practical implementation of the organisational processes of the EOI unit, in particular taking account of any significant changes to the volume of incoming EOI requests, to ensure that they are sufficient for effective EOI in practice.</td></tr>
</table>

Annex 1: Jurisdiction's response to the review report[14]

The Kingdom of the Government of Lesotho would like to thank the Peer Review Group for the review and most importantly the team of assessors for their dedication and insightful guidance during the review. The report is a reflection of the economic situation in Lesotho and the practical implementation of the international standard for transparency and exchange of information.

The recommendations have been noted and Lesotho is determined to act on them for further improvements in its exchange of information framework and practice. Following the Phase 1 review, a number of changes were implemented ranging from updating of forms, practices and development of Exchange of Information manual and function within the revenue authority. While there is still a lot of work to be done, Lesotho is grateful for these improvements that have been initiated through the work of the Global Forum.

With this said, Lesotho would once again like to reiterate is continuing commitment to the global standard.

14. This Annex presents the jurisdiction's response to the review report and shall not be deemed to represent the Global Forum's views.

Annex 2: List of Lesotho's exchange of information mechanisms

Multilateral and bilateral exchange of information agreements

- Lesotho signed the AMATM on 15 May 2014 and deposited its instrument of ratification on 7 October 2014. The AMATM has not yet entered into force in Lesotho. It will only enter into force 30 days after five member states submit their instrument of ratification. The AMATM is opened to all the African Tax Administration Forum members to sign. Not all members have signed the agreement. The status of the AMATM as at April 2016 is set out in the table below.
- Lesotho signed the Southern African Development Community Agreement on Assistance in Tax Matters ("SADC Agreement") on 18 August 2012 and deposited its instrument of ratification on 7 October 2014. The SADC Agreement has not yet entered into force in Lesotho. It will only enter into force 30 days after two thirds of the Southern African Development Community member states submit their instrument of ratification. Not all SADC members have signed the agreement. The status of the SADC Agreement as at April 2016 is set out in the table below.
- Lesotho has signed five DTAs and two TIEAs. Three of the five DTAs and the two TIEAs are in force.

Table of Lesotho's exchange of information relations

The table below summarises Lesotho's EOI relations with individual jurisdictions. These relations allow for exchange of information upon request in the field of direct taxes. The AMATM and SADC Agreement have not yet entered into force.

No.	Jurisdiction	Type of EOI agreement	Date signed	Date in force
1	Botswana	DTA	20-Apr-2010	Not yet in force
		SADC Agreement	18-Aug-2012	Not yet in force
2	Democratic Republic of the Congo	SADC Agreement	18-Aug-2012	Not yet in force
3	Guernsey	TIEA	3-Jul-2013	3-Jan-2015
4	Isle of Man	TIEA	16-Sep-2013	3-Jan-2015
5	Malawi	SADC Agreement	18-Aug-2012	Not yet in force
6	Mauritius	DTA	29-Aug-1997	9-Sep-2004
		SADC Agreement	18-Aug-2012	Not yet in force
7	Mozambique	AMATM	07-Nov-2014	Not yet in force
		SADC Agreement	18-Aug-2012	Not yet in force
8	Seychelles	DTA	5-Sep-2011	Not yet in force
		SADC Agreement	18-Aug-2012	Not yet in force
9	South Africa	DTA	18-Sep-2014	27-May-2016
		AMATM	1-Sep-2013	Not yet in force
		SADC Agreement	18-Aug-2012	Not yet in force
10	Swaziland	SADC Agreement	18-Aug-2012	Not yet in force
11	Tanzania	SADC Agreement	18-Aug-2012	Not yet in force
12	Uganda	AMATM	26-Mar-2014	Not yet in force
13	United Kingdom	DTA	29-Jan-1997	1-Jan-1998
14	Zambia	SADC Agreement	18-Aug-2012	Not yet in force

Annex 3: List of all laws, regulations and other relevant material

Commercial laws

Companies Act 2011

Companies Regulations 2012

Partnership Proclamation No. 78 of 1957

Friendly Societies Act, Act 7 of 1882

Societies Act 1966

Legal Practitioners Act 1983

Taxation laws

Income Tax Act 1993, updated up to 1 April 2012

Income Tax Explanatory Memorandum 1993

Revenue Appeals Tribunal Act 2005

Banking laws

Central Bank of Lesotho Act 2000

Financial Institutions Act 2012

Anti-money laundering laws

Financial Institutions (Know Your Customer) Guidelines 2007

Money Laundering and Proceeds of Crime Act 2008

Money Laundering (Accountable Institutions) Guidelines 2013

Annex 4: List of persons interviewed during the onsite visit

Ministry of Finance

Lesotho Revenue Authorities

- Commissioner General
- Legal and Policy Division
- International Treaty Development Section
- Operations Division (Audit)
- Investigations Unit

Registrar of Companies

Registrar of Deeds

Central Bank

Financial Intelligence Unit

ORGANISATION FOR ECONOMIC CO-OPERATION AND DEVELOPMENT

The OECD is a unique forum where governments work together to address the economic, social and environmental challenges of globalisation. The OECD is also at the forefront of efforts to understand and to help governments respond to new developments and concerns, such as corporate governance, the information economy and the challenges of an ageing population. The Organisation provides a setting where governments can compare policy experiences, seek answers to common problems, identify good practice and work to co-ordinate domestic and international policies.

The OECD member countries are: Australia, Austria, Belgium, Canada, Chile, the Czech Republic, Denmark, Estonia, Finland, France, Germany, Greece, Hungary, Iceland, Ireland, Israel, Italy, Japan, Korea, Latvia, Luxembourg, Mexico, the Netherlands, New Zealand, Norway, Poland, Portugal, the Slovak Republic, Slovenia, Spain, Sweden, Switzerland, Turkey, the United Kingdom and the United States. The European Union takes part in the work of the OECD.

OECD Publishing disseminates widely the results of the Organisation's statistics gathering and research on economic, social and environmental issues, as well as the conventions, guidelines and standards agreed by its members.

OECD PUBLISHING, 2, rue André-Pascal, 75775 PARIS CEDEX 16
(23 2016 44 1 P) ISBN 978-92-64-26613-1– 2016

www.ingramcontent.com/pod-product-compliance
Lightning Source LLC
Chambersburg PA
CBHW041324210926
51847CB00003B/42
* 9 7 8 9 2 6 4 2 6 6 1 3 1 *